SECRET
TWIN CITIES

A GUIDE TO THE WEIRD, WONDERFUL, AND OBSCURE

Julie Jo Severson

Lisa! Much appreciated. :)
Hopefully we can all
explore freely & safely
in the near future.
Julie Jo Severson

Reedy Press
PO Box 5131
St. Louis, MO 63139
www.reedypress.com

Library of Congress Control Number: 2019952738
ISBN: 9781681062600

Design by Jill Halpin
Unless otherwise indicated, all photos are courtesy of the author
or in the public domain.

Full color insert photos courtesy of Debra Bernard Photography.

Printed in the United States of America
20 21 21 23 24   5 4 3 2 1

CONTENTS

ACKNOWLEDGMENTS

Thank you to Reedy Press for offering me this super cool opportunity. To Julie Burton, founder of ModernWell—a local coworking, writing, and wellness center—for steering me toward this project and bringing out the best in everyone around her. To the fabulous Thursday afternoon ModernWell Writing Studio crew for weekly accountability, rallying, and so much more. To my talented friend Debra Bernard for joining me on several occasions to take the full color photos featured in the center insert. And to the countless locals and history buffs who expanded my universe this past year by sharing their diverse experiences and perspectives.

But most of all, thank you to my husband, Mike, for endless support and encouragement on the home front. And to Audrey, Caleb, and Amanda for putting up with my obscure little "field trips" while trusting me to not publish or post anything too exceedingly weird.

INTRODUCTION

Thousands of years ago, melting glaciers and an ancient waterfall began carving the way for the eventual development of two great cities on the banks of the upper Mississippi. Although one grew up mostly on the east side of the river and the other mostly on the west side, the two cities became tagged as twins.

We all know that "twins" is a bit of a misnomer, though. For one thing, Minneapolis is cosmopolitan while Saint Paul prefers a more laid-back, old-world existence. But as you get to know each city's unique endeavors and little-known spots, it's clear their gene pools are equally extraordinary and quirky.

Of course, cities are nothing without their people. As you read through the vignettes in the pages ahead, you'll gain glimpses of all kinds of folks, from early immigrants walking with suitcases through a hidden tunnel, to creatives pouring their souls into giant sculptures, to beer lovers sitting on stools buying $1 meat raffle tickets, to Jane Austen fans taking selfies with a life-size cutout of Colin Firth. Heck, you might even get a glimpse of yourself.

I've called the Twin Cities home most of my life, but I've never truly appreciated the wealth of history and hidden gems to be found here, until now. This guidebook, which includes the surrounding suburbs, stems from a year's worth of researching, circling destinations on my big crinkly map, taking exits I've never taken, exploring new and familiar places for a closer look, reaching out to local experts from archivists to bartenders, and finally learning the backstories of places and oddities I've driven by countless times.

I'm no Twin Cities know-it-all, but one thing I know for certain is this: it's impossible to run out of stuff to marvel over and be surprised about in this two-for-one metropolis.

WONDERLAND OFF I-35

Where is there an antique park that may look like a junkyard to some but is a Hollywood haven to others?

While driving toward the Twin Cities on I-35 heading north near Lakeville, you may have noticed a changing assortment of oddities atop a slight hill to your right. One day there may be a rocket ship, mechanical shark, and Big Top Ten Circus trailer. Another day there may be a submarine and a clunky old police paddy wagon.

Because life is busy, most of us will keep on driving rather than take the next exit (Exit 81) to investigate. But if you do take the exit and eventually find the narrow gravel road to Hot Sam's Antiques, you'll realize what a marvelous mishmash you would've missed if you hadn't.

Built in 1985 by Bobbie "Jake" Hood, a scrap collector and recycler, Hot Sam's is a ten-acre labor of love. Or as Jake calls it, "a junkyard with a sense of humor." He built the theme park as a wonderland for his mother, Gladys. Nicknamed Hot Sam, Gladys was also an avid scrap collector (not to mention a record-breaking race car driver). She later cared for her husband, who had suffered brain damage. Gladys passed away in 2010, but Jake keeps the park going in her honor with the help of his significant other, Kat; their dog, Alley-Oop; and resident artist, Barry.

Scattered throughout the woods and around the little antique shop are countless props, many placed in scenes that look like they belong in Hollywood—such as a top-secret area

When you don't take the time to check things out, you miss the Hot Sam's of the world—an antique theme park, or as the owner calls it, "a junkyard with a sense of humor."

HOT SAM'S ANTIQUES & FOTO PARK

WHAT Equal parts photo park, theme park, artist haven, junkyard, and antique shop

WHERE 22820 Pillsbury Ave., Lakeville (From the south, take I-35 Exit 81; from the north, take I-35 Exit 76)

COST Admission is free, but to keep the park going, there is a photo fee: smartphones, $10; cameras, $25. Every item at the park is for sale or rent (except for the ginormous Hardware Hank sign).

PRO TIP Closed in the winter.

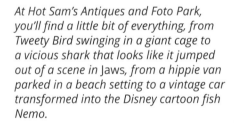

At Hot Sam's Antiques and Foto Park, you'll find a little bit of everything, from Tweety Bird swinging in a giant cage to a vicious shark that looks like it jumped out of a scene in Jaws, *from a hippie van parked in a beach setting to a vintage car transformed into the Disney cartoon fish Nemo.*

featuring aliens and a UFO. One day, the crew for *Grumpy Old Men* (filmed in the Twin Cities in 1993) came along and rented some antique chairs. The late, lovable Walter Matthau, who starred in the film, wanted the chairs for his own use after the filming was complete. According to Jake, Matthau thought he could simply walk off the set with the chairs. But Jake kindly told him, "Here in Minnesota, we have to pay for things."

SIDEWALK HARP

What's that wavy, light-up thing behind Target Field?

There's nothing like a curvaceous, glow-in-the-dark, musical sidewalk railing to boost your happy hormones. The forty-foot-long structure is located a short walk from the light rail stop by Target Field. It was designed by Jen Lewin, a light and interactive sculptor from New York City. When pedestrians wave their hands or move their bodies below it, perhaps on the way to work or a sporting event, sensors capped with LEDs are triggered. Like plucked strings, the sensors illuminate the landscape with an ensemble of sound and color.

The purpose of *Sidewalk Harp*, as Lewin calls it, is to inspire connection and lightheartedness between strangers passing by on the street. That echoes what goes on inside the tall glass building behind it for which it was designed: the headquarters for Be The Match, the National Marrow Donor Program.

Launched in 1986 from a tiny office at the American Red Cross in Saint Paul, Be The Match helps patients with leukemia, lymphoma, and other diseases who need a blood stem cell transplant. It now manages the largest and most diverse hematopoietic cell registry in the world. To date, the nonprofit has facilitated more than ninety-two thousand blood stem cell transplants.

The same artist also created an upcoming public artwork called *Aurora*, designed for the ticketing and baggage claim levels of Terminal 1-Lindbergh at Minneapolis–Saint Paul International

With its headquarters in Minneapolis, Be The Match is the world's largest and most diverse donor registry. It facilitates nearly sixty-two hundred blood stem cell transplants a year.

The Sidewalk Harp *in front of the grand glass entrance for Be The Match brings people together as it lights up the street with a symphony of color and sound.*

Airport. You'll know it when you see a giant half-spiral curving downward from the ticketing area to the baggage level. At the base, a cluster of glass representing Minnesota lakes changes colors when people stand on it. If people wave their hands, *Aurora* gently lights up with colors that change according to the seasons. Installation is scheduled to begin in fall 2020.

BE THE MATCH
SIDEWALK HARP

WHAT A light-up musical instrument that is part of the sidewalk in front of the headquarters for the National Marrow Donor Program

WHERE 500 N. Fifth St., Minneapolis

COST Free

PRO TIP Experiencing the *Sidewalk Harp* is best at night, of course. It's a great way to wrap up a romantic evening in downtown Minneapolis.

JAMES J. HILL STAIRS OF PAIN

Where can you get a killer workout on a century-old staircase built by one of America's greatest entrepreneurs and his son?

James J. Hill, a Canadian-born Minnesotan of iron will, worked furiously to take the Great Northern Railway from the Twin Cities across the Rockies to Seattle. Known as the Empire Builder, he contributed to the rise of Minnesota industry perhaps more than any other person.

For twenty-five years, Hill, his wife, and their ten children lived in a rugged thirty-six-thousand-square-foot, five-floor stone mansion along the distinguished Summit Avenue in Saint Paul. However, for fitness enthusiasts (or gluttons for punishment), the best part is the steep, outdoor staircase next to it that leads to Irvine Avenue below.

Saint Paul has many wonderful public stairways. But this

WALNUT STREET STAIRCASE

WHAT The public staircase between the James J. Hill House and the former home of Hill's son Louis

WHERE Between 240 and 260 Summit Ave. W., Saint Paul

COST Free to climb the steps; mansion tour, $6–$10

PRO TIP Sunday is self-guided-tour day at the mansion.

At the time of railroad magnate James J. Hill's funeral in 1916, every train and steamship of the Great Northern came to a stop for five minutes to honor him. You can also honor his legacy by climbing up and down what some fitness groups call the James J. Hill Stairs of Pain.

When looking down the steep, hidden staircase between the two homes, the James J. Hill mansion is to the immediate left and the former mansion of Hill's son Louis is to the immediate right.

particular one, which includes roughly two hundred steps, offers a storied past and one of the city's most spectacular views. Some who use the steps for their workouts call them the James J. Hill Stairs of Pain. But the actual name is the Walnut Street Steps.

According to Larry Millet's *AIA Guide to the Twin Cities*, Walnut was once a platted street there. But in 1901, Hill's son Louis (who was hugely instrumental in developing Glacier National Park) negotiated an easement to vacate the street so he could build a mansion next door to his dad's. As part of the deal, the city asked Hill to build a staircase that would forever be open to the public.

The staircase is bordered by a wall that is stonework on the James J. Hill side and red brick on the Louis Hill side. At one time, there were two doors from the staircase onto the James J. Hill property, possibly meant for cooks and servants. When you walk the stairs, look closely and you'll see the outlines where they were filled in.

UNDERGROUND LIBRARY

Where is the world's largest collection of Sherlock Holmes books stored in a two-story underground vault?

Even in this digital age, interacting with the pages, bindings, and jackets of tangible, old-fashioned books is pure bliss for bookworms and archivists. And nowhere is there a more ambitious effort to protect and preserve them from warping, fading, or burning than at the Elmer L. Andersen Library.

Named after the thirtieth governor of Minnesota, the library is located high on the river bluffs on the West Bank of the University of Minnesota. Built beneath it are the library's two geology-friendly caverns. Each cavern is two stories high and as long as two football fields. And they're loaded with treasures. While driving below on West River Parkway, you may notice a giant arched portal tucked into the bluff. It looks like a secret military defense site. But it's actually the back-door delivery entrance to the caverns.

One of those caverns holds 1.5 million books and is a shared storage facility for Twin Cities campus libraries and other libraries around the state. The other cavern contains rare books and archives, including collections of university memories, the state's history of human rights advocacy, records documenting the emergence of the computer industry, Pulitzer Prize clippings, children's literature, Minnesota Orchestra papers, and even the world's largest collection of Sherlock Holmes books.

Behind the big doors are huge environmentally controlled underground caverns, holding and preserving volumes of written treasures.

This is the back-door delivery entrance to the University of Minnesota's Elmer L. Andersen Library storage vaults. It's not the school's only underground facility, though. The Civil Engineering Building is 95 percent underground. And its High Energy Physics Lab, located in an old iron mine in northern Minnesota, is 2,341 feet beneath the surface.

UNDERGROUND CAVERNS BELOW U OF M ANDERSEN LIBRARY

WHAT Massive underground library storage caverns

WHERE Elmer L. Andersen Library, 222 Twenty-First Ave. S., Minneapolis

COST Free

PRO TIP Tours of the caverns are available after each of the library's First Fridays programs (first Friday of the month, October–December and February–May, at noon).

The subterranean storage structures were created in 2000 by excavating nearly one hundred thousand cubic yards of sandstone and shale from the bluffs of the Mississippi River, right below the main library. They are sealed from the outside elements and equipped with a special ventilation system, timed lighting, and flood-protection pumps. Considered ideal conditions for preserving paper, film, and videotape, the caverns are maintained at 62 degrees Fahrenheit and approximately 50 percent relative humidity.

STER GIFT EXCHANGE

What did Saint Paul receive from its sister city in China in exchange for embellished Snoopy and Lucy statues?

Cities throughout the world have been pledging themselves as lifelong "sisters" since the 1950s. That's when President Dwight Eisenhower launched Sister Cities International, an organization that promotes peace and prosperity between cultures. In 2018, Saint Paul and one of its sister cities— Changsha, China—celebrated their thirtieth "sibling" anniversary with a rather interesting gift exchange.

Changsha presented Saint Paul with the Xiang Jiang Pavilion, a replica of China's famous Aiwan Pavilion. In return, through the efforts of the Minnesota China Friendship Garden Society, Saint Paul gave Changsha five statues depicting characters from the *Peanuts* comic strip created and made famous by Saint Paul native Charles M. Schulz (see "Oh, Good Grief," page 160). One of the statues portrayed Lucy wearing a traditional Hmong dress. Another was a Snoopy doghouse with Minnesota state symbols painted in a Chinese brush style.

The *Peanuts* statues are now installed at Changsha's Yanghu Wetlands Park Science Museum. The pavilion is now the focal point of America's first-ever Changsha-style China garden, located north of the picnic pavilion at Phalen Regional Park. Officially named the Saint Paul–Changsha China Friendship

---

The China Friendship Garden is meant to honor not only Minnesota's thirty-five thousand Chinese immigrants and their descendants but also the eighty thousand Hmong who live in the state and claim Changsha, China, as their ancestral home.

The Minnesota China Friendship Garden Society worked closely with the Saint Paul Department of Parks & Recreation and Changsha Hunan Jianke Landscaping Company on the concept, design, and construction of this China Friendship Garden. It's the first Changsha-style garden in the United States.

CHINA FRIENDSHIP GARDEN

WHAT A calm oasis featuring a pavilion gifted from Saint Paul's sister city—Changsha, China

WHERE Phalen Regional Park, 1600 Phalen Dr., Saint Paul

COST Free

PRO TIP While at Phalen Regional Park, look for the nine-foot *Meditation* sculpture by Changsha sculptor Master Lei Yixin near the picnic shelter. It was one of the reasons Phalen Regional Park was selected for the China Friendship Garden.

Garden of Whispering Willows and Flowing Waters, the garden is a year-round oasis of weeping willows, lakes, streams, and decorative pathways.

Made of granite and wood, the pavilion was built in China before it was disassembled, packed, and shipped to Saint Paul. Local construction workers teamed with Chinese artisans to reassemble it on-site. Also featured at the park is the Hmong Heritage Wall, which is a pink granite sculpture adorned with cultural symbols like butterflies, necklaces, and musical instruments representing the Minnesota Hmong and Hunan Hmong cultures. Plans are in the works for adding a classroom pavilion, an arched bridge, and a Hmong Cultural Plaza.

LOST AND FOUND

Where do objects go when they're missing?

There are a number of theories about what happens to things we can't find. Maybe we don't look hard enough. Maybe gnomes steal them when we're not looking. Maybe they get sucked up by black holes or the Bermuda Triangle. Or maybe some of them end up at Center for Lost Objects (CFLO) in Saint Paul. If they do, there's a good chance they'll be repurposed.

"I love to find new life for people's loved things," says owner Amy Buchanan. Buchanan, by the way, is also a local singer who reintroduced Le Cirque Rouge—a performance group that mixes live music, comedy, and burlesque—to the Twin Cities in 2003.

CFLO is a haven for oddball treasure seekers. Looking for a duck lamp with a toupee? How about porcupine quill earrings? Mechanical wind-up bunnies in mint condition? A crate of empty Coke bottles? Five-foot angel wings? Doll heads? A light-up robot? A taxidermy squirrel? It's not all a bunch of misfits, though. There are also beautiful antiques, craft items, and home decor, often brought in by family members who are in the process of sorting through a loved one's belongings after they've passed away or transitioned into a care facility.

One family brought in their mother's cedar chest filled with vintage linens, some dating back to the 1920s. They also brought in seven hundred pounds of jewelry she'd purchased from church sales. Another patron brought in twenty boxes of stunning black and white eight-by-ten photos taken by a family

---

Follow the path of curiosity (or Seventh Street West) to Center for Lost Objects in Saint Paul. You're probably not going to find your sunglasses or keys there, but get ready to peruse a world of oddball items and rare collectibles.

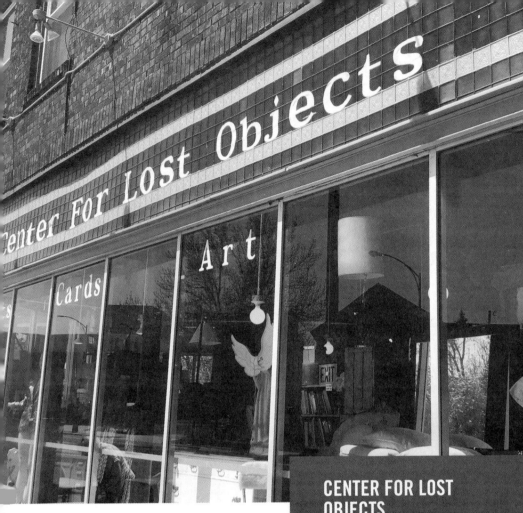

The shop's large front window doubles as a stage for musicians, as well as live models who pose for on-site drawing sessions using the store's quirky items as props.

member who had worked as a German darkroom technician and for the American Red Cross. Buchanan also uses her shop to host performances, pop-up shops, classes on how to recycle old furniture, and a drawing club that uses live models posing with the store's items as props.

CENTER FOR LOST OBJECTS

WHAT Open art studio, curiosity shop, and gallery

WHERE 957 Seventh St. W., Saint Paul

COST Price tags range from a few bucks to several thousand dollars.

PRO TIP Up the road is the fantastic Keg and Case West Seventh Market in the old Schmidt Brewery keg house.

IN THE SHADOWS

Who are those shadowy figures at the end of Nicollet Mall?

Nicollet Mall, the first transit mall in the nation, has long been the heart of downtown Minneapolis. To enhance the walking experience, a $50 million renovation was completed in 2018 that included more trees, colorful seating, LED lights, lanterns, new art displays, and reinstallment of previous displays. Perhaps the most underappreciated artwork of all is *Shadows of Spirit*, a cluster of seven distorted bronze shadows first set into the pavement between Eleventh and Grant streets in 1992.

Shadows of Spirit was commissioned by the City of Minneapolis and created by visual artists Seitu Jones and Ta-coumba Aiken. The poetic text embedded within the shadows was written by Soyini Guyton. Local writer Regina Flanagan interviewed the artists for a new website and blog (nicolletmallart.org) managed by the city's Art in Public Places program.

SHADOWS OF SPIRIT

WHAT A series of shadowy figures embedded into pavement on Nicollet Mall

WHERE Between Eleventh and Grant streets on Nicollet Mall, Minneapolis

COST Free

PRO TIP Seitu Jones and Ta-coumba Aiken recently collaborated on another set of shadows for the sidewalks at the Minneapolis Sculpture Garden.

According to Flanagan's interview, Jones and Aiken created the shadow outlines by first taking photos of people walking on Nicollet Mall during four specific times of year: the winter solstice, spring equinox, summer solstice, and fall equinox. In her blog writings, Flanagan reports that the shadows honor seven people who represent a vital part of the city's history.

Those seven people include *Nellie Stone Johnson*, a union organizer and the first black elected official in Minneapolis;

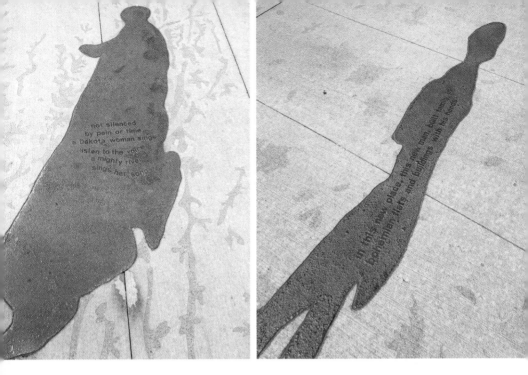

Before they were temporarily removed for construction, the orientation of each of the seven Shadows of Spirit *on Nicollet Mall was carefully documented so it could be returned to the same orientation later.*

Woo Yee Sing, an early Chinese immigrant; *an unnamed Eastern European immigrant settler* of the Bohemian Flats located on the west bank of the Mississippi; *Meridel Le Sueur*, a twentieth-century writer and community activist; *Dred Scott*, an African American man who was enslaved and sued the Supreme Court for his freedom and the freedom of his wife, Harriet Robinson; *an unnamed labor striker*; and *Anpetu Sapa Win* (Black Day Woman), a member of the Dakota who, according to legend, took her life by paddling a canoe over St. Anthony Falls.

"The *Shadows of Spirit* series on Nicollet Mall honors the contributions of Minneapolis's first change-makers, their ancestors, and all who have contributed to the rich life of Minnesota." (Source: Minneapolis interactive map: cityoflakes.maps.arcgis.com.)

REVERENCE FOR ROCK

Where and why is there a face overlooking Saint Paul?

Since 2006, there's been a big but unobtrusive face keeping watch over the city of Saint Paul. It stands guard from the edge of a quiet neighborhood above Wabasha Caves. The nine-foot, two-and-a-half-ton structure, named *Overlook*, was created by local resident David Wyrick. He carved it out of a ten-ton square block of dolomitic limestone.

Wyrick was one of fourteen stone carvers from around the world who came together for six weeks on the lawn of Saint Paul College during a 2006 International Stone Carving Symposium called Minnesota Rocks! Using blocks of stone donated by Minnesota quarries, the artists created a dozen sculptures for placement in public places throughout Saint Paul.

Wyrick's original plan was to create two identical faces like bookends. But he had a heck of a time splitting his big block of limestone into two. It didn't end up cracking in the direction he wanted, so he settled for one face with a long neck. Some of the other sculptures produced during the symposium include an Ojibwa woman holding a sacred bowl at Indian Mounds Regional Park, a rock filled with paving stones representing memory at Boyd Park, protective sentinels that stand across from the Temple of Aaron, and the sculpture known as *Meditation* at Phalen Regional Park.

Minnesota stone is prized all over the country. It's used in many of the monuments and museums on the National Mall in Washington and in buildings around the Mount Rushmore monument.

Tucked into a quiet neighborhood above Wabasha Caves, you'll find the face made of Minnesota stone turned away from the street and overlooking downtown Saint Paul.

The sculptures serve as a reminder of the beauty of Minnesota's natural resources. But the cultural exchange that took place between the stone carvers from Minnesota, Mexico, Italy, Zimbabwe, China, Japan, Germany, Finland, and Egypt was just as important. Despite language barriers, new friendships were formed while they shared their deep reverence for rock and helped one another drill and pound.

MINNESOTA ROCKS!

WHAT Twelve stone carvings on permanent display throughout Saint Paul

WHERE The face sculpture is at the corner of Prospect Boulevard and Stryker Avenue, Saint Paul. Other Minnesota Rocks! locations and artists are posted at publicartstpaul.org.

COST Free

PRO TIP Minnesota is home to some of the oldest rocks on the planet. Check out the website of the Minnesota Department of Natural Resources to learn more.

THE HOLLOW

Where is there an old white tunnel that leads to a park hidden below street level? And why is the park the subject of an opera?

East of downtown Saint Paul is an old white tunnel that leads to a lush, exceedingly quiet eighteen-acre valley with soaring cliffs hiding it from the rest of the city. Looming above on the north is the sprawling old Hamm's Brewery. For nearly one hundred years, from the 1860s to the 1950s, the area was home to one of the oldest working-class immigrant settlements in Minnesota. Early inhabitants named it "Svenska Dalen" or Swede Hollow.

First came the Swedes and Poles. Later came Italians and Mexicans. At one point, there were close to a thousand people living down there in a variety of shanties. They'd arrive by train, walk along the tracks from Union Depot, and enter through that tunnel.

There was no electricity. No plumbing. No stores. The creek was their sewer, with easily tipped outhouses propped over it on stilts. Some viewed the area as a wretched slum. Others simply knew it as home: a place where neighbors from different cultures came together to share coffee and bread, smoke pipes under the moon, and fall asleep to the rhythmic rattling of trains. "It was the best place to be . . . I'll never regret starting my life down there," said former Swede Hollow resident Mike Sanchelli during a PBS *Lost Twin Cities* video segment.

Swede Hollow, now an enchanting park, is so serene you nearly forget there's a city above it. You can almost feel the spirits of all those who once settled there in rustic shanties while rebuilding their lives.

This tucked-away pedestrian tunnel was once the only way to enter Swede Hollow, a lush valley hidden below street level that served as an immigrant shantytown for nearly one hundred years. A few remnants from those days are still visible.

In December 1956, the city declared the area a health hazard. The last fourteen families were evicted and the remaining dwellings burned down by the Saint Paul Fire Department. In the 1970s, it was cleaned up and dedicated as a nature center thanks to the efforts of East Side residents and the Saint Paul Garden Club. The poignant story of Swede Hollow has provoked a number of books and theater productions. In 2012, composer Ann Millikan premiered an opera named *Swede Hollow*.

SWEDE HOLLOW PARK

WHAT A hidden ravine that used to be home to one of Minnesota's oldest immigrant settlements

WHERE Original white tunnel (shown in the photo) that leads to the park is located just south of the Hope Academy campus (720 Payne Ave., Saint Paul)

COST Free

PRO TIP You can also enter the park through the historic Seventh Street Improvement Arches (see image in the center insert), accessed from the Bruce Vento Regional Trail.

EMPTRESS OF TEAS

Where can you channel your inner Jane Austen while learning about loose leaf tea?

Although it's been more than two hundred years since her most celebrated novel, *Pride and Prejudice*, was published, Jane Austen still inspires huge devotion. Her narratives—brimming with razor-sharp wit, universal themes of love and status, and the rich interior lives of female characters—keep resonating through the ages. And so do her countless scenes with people drinking tea.

It's with those two passions—Jane Austen and fine tea—that Julia Matson launched Bingley's Tea House, a loose leaf tea retail boutique hidden in the Minneapolis Whittier neighborhood. Tea workshops, events with local authors, and tea talks are also offered. Matson, "The Temptress of Teas," is a graduate of New York's Specialty Tea Institute and a lifetime member of the Jane Austen Society.

Venture inside the unmarked Tanek Building on the corner of Twenty-Sixth Street and Stevens Avenue, go to the second floor, and you'll find your way. One end of the quaint shop, next to the beautiful windows with draped curtains, is dedicated to the elegance of a Jane Austen novel. It even has a tea-stained couch from Britain and a life-size cutout of Colin Firth (a.k.a Mr. Darcy). On the other end is an area dedicated to Gong Fu Cha–style tea inspired by Matson's world travels to tea farms.

It is a truth universally acknowledged that Jane Austen pairs well with tea, and there's no better place to do so than at Bingley's Tea House.

Bingley's Tea House is a small, woman-owned tea shop inspired by a love of fine loose leaf tea and Jane Austen. It's a true gem tucked away in the heart of Minneapolis on the second floor of an unmarked building with pretty windows.

Matson's main brand is a Jane Austen Tea Series, specifically blended to match the personality traits of Austen's characters, with names like "Compassion for Mrs. Bennet's Nerves" and "Lydia Has More Fun." Her products can also be found online and at a growing number of local restaurants and coffee shops by the cup or blended into cocktails. She also sells bath bombs infused with her tea (because, of course, Jane Austen is the bomb!).

BINGLEY'S TEA HOUSE

WHAT A tea house featuring Jane Austen and Gong Fu Cha–inspired teas

WHERE In the Tanek Building, 118 E. Twenty-Sixth St., Ste. 208, Minneapolis

COST Teas, $6–$15

PRO TIP Bingley's is open on Saturdays and for special events and private parties. Check janeaustenteas.com for updates.

LANDMARK LEGENDS AND LETTERS

Where can you view a rare collection of handwritten letters by famous composers in the same building where a notorious gangster was once chained to a radiator?

The castle-like Landmark Center in Saint Paul's core has long been a laboratory of fascinating history. Completed in 1902, it originally housed the Federal Courts and Post Office. Today it's a cultural haven.

It's where US Representative Andrew Volstead penned the 1919 National Prohibition Act from his office on the third floor. It's where the kidnapping of millionaire William Hamm Jr. was investigated by the FBI in Room 203. It's where gangster Alvin "Creepy" Karpis was allegedly chained to a radiator for three days in Room 323 before his trial. It's where Rose Pastor Stokes's appeal of her treason conviction for her critical newspaper letter to the editor was heard in Court Room 408. And according to urban myth, it's also where the ghost of former Hollyhocks Club owner Jack Pfeiffer still hangs out in the ladies' restrooms.

Today, much of the second floor is dedicated to the Schubert Club Museum. Founded in 1882, Schubert Club is one of the oldest arts organizations in the country and

---

"To me, everything is cold, cold as ice. Perhaps if you were with me, I might possibly take more pleasure in the kindness of people I meet here . . ." (Excerpt from a letter from Mozart to his wife, September 30, 1790)

After government agencies moved out, the Landmark Center fell into disrepair and was in danger of being torn down. Fortunately, in 1972, a group of citizens began restoring the building to its former grandeur. Check out the extraordinary music museum on the second floor.

is credited with bringing virtually all of the world's great recitalists to Saint Paul. At the museum, visitors step back in time through a gallery of centuries-old keyboards, music boxes, phonographs, and a rare collection of one hundred original handwritten letters by famous composers.

The letters are displayed on a rotating basis with about a dozen at a time. Audio narrations of select letters allow you to listen along. Beethoven complains about being poisoned. Chopin grumbles about his finances. Mozart reassures his wife (this letter is by far the most endearing and is on display most of the time). The letters were donated by Gilman Ordway, the grandson of Lucius Pond Ordway, for whom the Ordway Center for the Performing Arts across the street was named.

LANDMARK CENTER AND SCHUBERT CLUB MUSEUM

WHAT The rich legacy of Landmark Center, including FBI investigations, sensational trials, and a legendary music museum

WHERE 75 Fifth St. W., Saint Paul

COST Free self-guided tours

PRO TIP The music museum is undergoing a renovation to include more hands-on, interactive activities. Check schubert.org for updates.

WHERE'S *SCHERZO*?

Whatever happened to the famous statue unveiled during the opening of the Foshay Tower?

In 1929, Wilbur B. Foshay realized a childhood dream by building a skyscraper in the image of the Washington Monument as headquarters for his utilities company. He even had every side of it embellished with his name in ten-foot-tall, light-up letters. Once the tallest building between Chicago and the West Coast, the Foshay Tower remains a beloved Minneapolis icon, now home to the W Minneapolis – The Foshay hotel.

To create a centerpiece for the courtyard, Foshay hired sculptress Harriet Frishmuth to cast a life-size nude nymph, dubbed *Scherzo*. The statue was unveiled during Foshay's opening extravaganza. Months later, however, the stock market crashed, and Foshay's empire toppled.

A few years later, after a tumultuous public trial, Foshay went to prison for conducting a shady pyramid scheme. He was soon pardoned by President Truman, though. Meanwhile, *Scherzo* was moved to the entrance of a former restaurant in downtown Minneapolis called Charlie's Café Exceptionale. Nurses from a nearby hospital occasionally draped clothes on her. But where did *Scherzo* go after Charlie's closed in 1982?

FOSHAY TOWER AND ITS FAMOUS STATUE

WHAT The whereabouts of *Scherzo*, a nude nymph statue made famous by the opening of the Foshay Tower

WHERE Calhoun Towers, 3430 List Pl.; Foshay Tower Museum and Observation Deck, 821 Marquette Ave. S., Minneapolis

COST Foshay Museum admission, $6–$10

PRO TIP Harriet Frishmuth created only one other full-size statue of *Scherzo*'s exact design, and it's at Ball State University. You'll find a different one of her designs at the Como Park Conservatory Sunken Garden.

Created in 1929 by Harriet Frishmuth as a centerpiece for the Foshay Tower courtyard, the original Scherzo *now stands in front of a tucked-away, high-rise apartment complex off Excelsior Boulevard.*

According to a 2011 episode of *Lost Twin Cities, Scherzo* was relocated to the now demolished Leamington Hotel and then to a private home. But what many people don't know is that since 2013, *Scherzo* has been frolicking in front of Calhoun Towers, a high-rise apartment tucked up on a hill off Excelsior Boulevard.

It was the late local millionaire Robert Short who purchased *Scherzo* after Charlie's closed. He owned Leamington Hotel. He also owned Calhoun Towers (and the Minneapolis Lakers before they moved to Los Angeles). After Short died, ownership of Calhoun Towers stayed in his family until it was purchased by Bader Development in 2016. The Short family still owns *Scherzo*, however. According to the new developer and Robert Short's son, Brian, there are no plans to move her.

Scherzo was first unveiled during the lavish 1929 opening of the Foshay Tower, featuring fireworks, dancing girls, complimentary gold watches, and music composed and conducted by John Philip Sousa (who wasn't very happy when William Foshay's check to him bounced).

NEON-LIT ISLAND

What's the story behind the island with the glow-in-the-dark beer sign standing on it?

The iconic Grain Belt Beer sign, oddly situated next to a Catholic high school, has loomed over the river and Minneapolis's downtown skyline since 1950. But most likely, even many locals haven't explored the tucked-away island on which it stands.

Nicollet Island is a forty-eight-acre parkland of trails, bridges, streetlamps, and preserved Victorian houses on cobbled streets that make you feel like you're in a time warp. Through the years, the island has been home to millionaires, monks, saw millers, hobos, hippies, drug dealers, artists, and a couple of donkeys named Pearl and Sheba.

Named after French explorer Joseph N. Nicollet, the island was first used as a birthing place by the Dakota. The roar of nearby St. Anthony Falls muted the mothers' cries, protecting them from enemies. In 1865, William Eastman and John Merriam gained ownership of the island and turned the southern end into an industrial complex and the northern end into a residential neighborhood. Read "Falls Fiasco," page 72, to learn how the pair's shenanigans nearly turned Minneapolis into a sinkhole in the process.

At some point, the island's character began to "unravel" a bit as hooligans from the former downtown skid row—a dense stretch of bars, flophouses, and homeless shelters—migrated there too. In efforts to clean the island up again, the Minneapolis Park & Recreation Board took control of most of the island in 1983. Ninety-nine-year leases were offered for $1

Nicollet Island, on the Mississippi River, is a quaint hidden treasure in the middle of the city.

The Grain Belt Beer bottle cap sign, which glows in the dark once again after a long hiatus, stands as a beloved landmark on Nicollet Island. The storied island is connected by trails and bridges to St. Anthony Main and Boom Island.

NICOLLET ISLAND

WHAT The only inhabited natural island on the Mississippi

WHERE If going by car, enter at East Island Avenue and Merriam Street, just before crossing Merriam Street Bridge into Saint Anthony Main.

COST Free

PRO TIP After exploring the island, wander down to the pedestrian bridge on the lower north end and cross over to Boom Island or to B. F. Nelson Park, which is right on a major bird migration route.

to individuals willing to renovate the deteriorated north-end homes to historic standards. Some homes were even moved there from other parts of Minneapolis.

GROWN-UP DIORAMAS

Where are some of the world's best and biggest wildlife museum exhibits made?

For most of us, our first experience with dioramas was the inside of a shoebox. Using construction paper, yarn, ribbons, scissors, glitter, and glue, we captured 3-D snapshots of our world in miniature. Then we carefully held our gloppy creation on our laps during the bumpy school bus ride and proudly presented it to our teacher.

You won't often hear a kid say, "I want to be a diorama maker when I grow up." But some actually do grow up to be one. In fact, a few of the world's most talented ones are employed in the Twin Cities at Blue Rhino Studio.

Blue Rhino is a custom exhibit design and fabrication firm that works with museums, zoos, and visitor centers all over the globe to create lifelike, nature-themed models and dioramas. The operation began in 1998 in President Tim Quady's garage. Today, it's housed inside a sixteen-thousand-square-foot warehouse in Eagan. If you've been to Bell Museum in its new building on the University of Minnesota Saint Paul campus, you've experienced the brilliant work of Blue Rhino Studio.

Bell Museum, first established in 1872 at the U of M's Minneapolis Campus, is chock-full of dioramas. Blue Rhino Studio created the newest and most gasp-worthy one: a Minnesota Ice Age diorama scene including an eleven-foot-tall woolly mammoth. After the mammoth's frame was fashioned out of foam and fiberglass, every teeny tiny inch of thick

---

How do you bring the world into a room? That's the goal for every diorama project. "There is no magic to it. It is talent and patience," says Tim Quady, president of Blue Rhino Studio.

The Blue Rhino Studio is the place where each hair was painstakingly glued onto Woolly Mammoth, now part of the Ice Age diorama at Bell Museum. Photo courtesy of Blue Rhino Studio.

hair was glued on by hand. *Star Wars* fans will be interested to know that the hair on Woolly Mammoth was sourced from the same supplier that made the Chewbacca costume.

BLUE RHINO STUDIO AND BELL MUSEUM

WHAT Creators of world-class diorama exhibits for museums and visitor centers

WHERE Blue Rhino Studio is not open to the public. Instead, go see their Woolly Mammoth creation at Bell Museum, 2088 Larpenteur Ave. W., Saint Paul

COST Bell Museum admission, $9–$12

PRO TIP Bell Museum also has a cool digital planetarium.

29

BILLS AND BOWLING BALLS

Why is the bar in this bowling alley covered in dollar bills? And how many bills are there?

As you descend into the cramped quarters of the Ran-Ham Bowling Center in Highland Park, your eyes might first gravitate to the wall murals featuring aliens spraying ketchup and mustard at each other. Next, you might marvel at the exposed pipes, large disco ball, and people still keeping score using paper and pencils. But it's the moment you walk into the bar next to the eight bowling lanes when you really know you've found a quirky gem. Not only is the bar built into a railroad car, but the ceiling and walls are smothered in dollar bills.

The first signed dollar bill was pinned up in 2010 during "$1 beer night" by a friend of the two owners, Ted Casper and Mike Runyon. The friend was leaving for a long trip and tried to leave Casper and Runyon a tip, but they refused it. According to Casper, the friend then said, "Well, okay, I plan to come back from my trip broke, so I'm going to sign and pin up a dollar that I can use when I get back."

That bill, which ignited a tradition that keeps on going, is now mounted on a plaque. How many bills are there? "Nobody has bothered to count," said the bartender on duty. He guessed maybe five to seven thousand. A guy sitting at the bar said he heard it was about sixteen thousand. "It's probably somewhere in between," said Casper.

It all started when a friend of the two owners tried to leave them a tip, but they refused to accept it. So she signed a dollar bill and pinned it up.

Ran-Ham Bowling Center is a one-of-a-kind, with whimsical murals, an old-fashioned pencil-and-paper scoring system, bowling balls older than your mother, and a bar that sits in an old train car and is covered with cash.

Casper and Runyon also own the Nook, the no-frills joint upstairs. The Nook is home to the "Nookie" burger—their version of the famous Juicy, or Jucy Lucy. If you're new to town, a Lucy is a burger with molten, bubbly cheese that oozes out of the patty. Locals have been arguing over how to spell it and which of two Minneapolis bars invented it (Matt's Bar, which spells it Jucy, or the 5-8 Club, which spells it Juicy) ever since it hit the food scene in the 1950s.

RAN-HAM BOWLING CENTER

WHAT Historic bowling alley featuring a bar covered with dollar bills

WHERE 492 Hamline Ave. S., Saint Paul

COST $4–$5; shoe rental $2

PRO TIP Casper and Runyon also own Shamrock's Irish Nook at 995 Seventh St. W., Saint Paul.

FEEL THE BEAT

Where can you participate in a women's drum circle, and how might it improve your immune system?

Modern research verifies that the sound of a beating drum reduces blood pressure, regulates heart rate, and may help treat a wide range of ailments from Parkinson's disease and Alzheimer's disease to anxiety and addiction. Not all that surprising when you think about it. Even before we're born, we're exposed to the calming rhythm of our mother's heartbeat from the womb. And there's no better place to re-create that heartbeat than at the Women's Drum Center (WDC) that's been tucked inside the Dow Building of Saint Paul for the past twenty years.

While there are some co-ed opportunities for men and for families to drum together at the WDC, the bulk of the classes offered are for women. Launched in an era when drumming was considered something that only men did, the center is a big, friendly space filled with all kinds of drums, rock shakers, colorful banners, and women celebrating their true selves as musicians, composers, teachers, and leaders.

Sit in on a class for just ten minutes, and you'll feel the stress of the day roll right off your body. The women, some in their bare feet, have the time of their lives jamming on drum sets and in African and Brazilian hand drum circles. More experienced drummers can try out for an ensemble called drumHeart (they use a capital H to emphasize Heart), which

Through drumming workshops for all levels at the Women's Drum Center, women are breaking free from old stereotypes while finding avenues to better health and healing.

For more than twenty years, the Women's Drum Center has been operating as a nonprofit in the Dow Building—home to a community of artists, from muralists and sculptors to metal workers and monster makers. This photo was taken during the Tuesday evening Women Who Groove *class.*

performs at events such as Race for the Cure, the Twin Cities AIDS Walk, the Headwaters Walk for Justice, and the State Fair.

WOMEN'S DRUM CENTER

WHAT World percussion programs that nurture, heal, and inspire

WHERE 2242 University Ave. W., Ste. B6, Saint Paul

COST Tuesday evening beginner class, $10 per session

PRO TIP Each fall, the center offers a week-long test drive event for folks to try out a class for free.

TANGLED TOWER

Where is there a soaring medieval water tower that people drive by all day long without seeing?

While Saint Paul's street patterns are irregular due to hills, bluffs, and the river winding through it, Minneapolis is mostly made up of straight-line grids. Except for Tangletown, a lovely labyrinth of winding, knotted streets that slopes down to Minnehaha Creek from Fiftieth Street between I-35W and Lyndale Avenue. Nestled in the heart of the tangle since 1932 is the Washburn Park Water Tower.

The 110-foot concrete cylinder is situated on a hill on a dead-end, shrouded by a dense residential area and tall trees. Unless you are within a block of it, you'd never know it was there. When it suddenly does come into sight—with wide, stately steps leading up to its base—the grandeur nearly takes your breath away.

Encircling the top of the tower are eight-foot-tall, five-ton eagles with spread wings ready for flight. Around the base are eighteen-foot-tall, eight-ton "guardians of health" holding a

The beautifully designed Washburn Park Water Tower was a joint effort of three highly skilled professionals from the neighborhood. They took it upon themselves to turn it into a one-of-a-kind treasure.

The Washburn Park Water Tower is a Medieval Revival structure built in 1932. Despite its massive size, it's completely hidden from view in a densely populated residential area until you're within a block of it.

perpetual vigil with swords. At a time when Minnesota was in the midst of a deadly typhoid outbreak, the guardians were symbolic protectors of the clean water supply.

Until the 1990s, the tower, with a capacity of 1.35 million gallons, provided water to the neighborhood. The tower was designed and engineered by three men from the neighborhood, including sculptor John K. Daniels, engineer William S. Hewitt, and lead architect Harry Wild Jones. Jones also designed the exquisite Memorial Chapel at Lakewood Cemetery.

EAST MEETS WEST

What is the significance of the zigzag bridge at the Lyndale Park Peace Garden?

Lyndale Park features some of Minneapolis's most beautiful gardens. One of them, the Peace Garden, located across from the illustrious rose garden, has been designated as an international peace site. Most visitors probably walk over its small zigzag bridge without knowing the story behind it.

In 1985, the Minneapolis Park Board invited local architect Jerry Allan to design a garden around a gift from Nagasaki, Japan. It was a single stone balustrade from Ground Zero of the atomic bomb detonated by the United States on August 6, 1945. Allan decided to build a zigzag bridge over a dry river bed after remembering a school lecture by Professor Heinrich Engel. Engel was a German submarine captain who moved to Japan at the end of World War II and taught architecture at the University of Minnesota in the 1960s. His lecture included the Japanese belief that evil spirits travel only in straight lines. The zigzag path prevents them from following people into the garden retreats.

After twenty years, the bridge wore out. The Park Board approached Allan, requesting a replacement. Allan invited his colleague Kinji Akagawa, a local artist originally from Japan, to embellish the new bridge. By this time, the city of Hiroshima had also sent a stone post. As Allan wrote in his journal, "Today the two posts rest in repose, at the head of each entry to the bridge, knowing they will never complete their path, while East truly

At the dedication of the zigzag bridge in 2009, architect Jerry Allan, local artist Kinji Akagawa, and other Twin Cities representatives met in the middle to shake hands with dignitaries from Nagasaki and Hiroshima.

While at Lyndale Park, take notice of the post found on each end of the zigzag bridge. They were found in the rubble of Ground Zero of the atomic bomb detonations in Hiroshima and Nagasaki. Also don't miss the beauty and significance of the Spirit of Peace *sculpture nearby.*

LYNDALE PARK PEACE GARDEN

WHAT Garden commemorating the detonation of atomic bombs in Hiroshima and Nagasaki, Japan, in 1945

WHERE Lyndale Park, 4124 Roseway Rd., Minneapolis

COST Free

PRO TIP Lyndale Park is located on the southwest segment of the Grand Rounds National Scenic Byway, a fifty-five-mile urban bike path within Minneapolis.

meets West at the center in Peace."

The Peace Garden also features a bronze sculpture known as the *Spirit of Peace*, designed by Caprice Glaser. It honors a Japanese girl who died from leukemia as a result of the bomb's radiation. She folded more than one thousand cranes before her death as a wish for peace. Each of the stones that surround the sculpture gives instructions for the next step in folding a paper crane.

37

OUR PRINCE

Why would a global megastar like Prince stay in the coldest metropolitan area in the continental United States?

Most world-famous musicians ditch their hometowns for music meccas like New York or Los Angeles. But not Prince. "I'm as much a part of the city where I grew up as I am anything," he once told *Minnesota Monthly*.

Minneapolis is where the prodigy grew up on the Northside playing basketball, attending church with his Aunt Mary, and intently watching his dad rehearse on the piano after returning from his day job molding plastic at Honeywell. When Prince was five, his mom (who had a wild streak) brought him to see his dad's jazz group—the Prince Rogers Trio—play for a burlesque show featuring scantily clad women dancing, singing, and screaming. Later he would refer to that event as one of the most influential musical experiences of his life.

While still a teen jamming with friends in Minneapolis's basements, attics, and the Way Community Center, Prince pioneered a new sound: a mix of R&B, funk, rock, and new wave the world had never heard before. After signing with Warner Bros. at age nineteen, he performed his first solo show at the Capri Theater in his old Northside neighborhood for $4.75 at the door. A few years later, he gave his landmark

---

"For the residents of Minneapolis, the loss of Prince is too large to describe. His music brought untold joy to people all over the world. But in Minneapolis, it is different. It is harder here . . ." (Former Minneapolis mayor Betsy Hodges)

This mural was painted by Rock "Cyfi" Martinez outside a property management company on the corner of Twenty-Sixth Street and Hennepin Avenue in Uptown Minneapolis soon after Prince's death. It features his love symbol, birth and death years, a white dove, and his sly, knowing expression accentuated with those deep eyes.

PRINCE AND MINNEAPOLIS

WHAT The transcendent bond between Prince and his hometown

WHERE For a self-guided digital history tour of Prince's Minneapolis, check out "Purple Places" at digitours.augsburg.edu.

COST Free

PRO TIP Also check the Preserve Minneapolis website for historical city tours, including an occasional guided walking tour of Prince places by local music historian Kristen Zschomler.

performance of "Purple Rain" at First Avenue, now emblazoned into a generation's brain.

As a global megastar who changed his name to an unpronounceable symbol to challenge unfair practices in the recording industry, Prince Rogers Nelson remade the sonic landscape. The whole world turned purple with grief when he was found dead on April 21, 2016, inside Paisley Park—his white aluminum paradise built in a cornfield of suburban Chanhassen. In Minneapolis, however, the loss was different and harder. As the grief has evolved over the years into celebrating his deep Minneapolis roots, it's apparent that Prince will forever be woven together with the city he called home.

ASSASSINATED PHOTO

Why are there two bullet holes in a photograph that hangs on the wall of a local German restaurant? And what's in the suitcase above the bar?

Eat Street, a section of Nicollet Avenue near Downtown Minneapolis well known for its wide variety of food options, has something for every craving. Looking for old-style Wiener schnitzel? Head to Black Forest Inn. The iconic eatery is steeped not only in authentic German fare but also in local art.

One notable piece is a large photo created, donated, and autographed by world-famous photographer Richard Avedon. It hangs on the wall in the bar area and features ten women at the 1963 Daughters of the American Revolution convention. Look closely, and you'll see two bullet holes: one in a woman's eye and another in a woman's abdomen.

The "assassin" was a regular at the bar named Ellis Miller Nelson. One day in February 1986, he was feeling a little ignored. So he stood up, pulled out his pistol, aimed toward the picture, and shot at it three times. (One of the shots somehow missed.) Chaos erupted and customers hid under tables. Nelson casually left the premises, walked to the nearby police station, and turned himself in.

The restaurant has been owned by the Christ family since 1965. They were concerned that nobody would want to come back after that incident. The next day it was packed as usual. The picture was never repaired. The wall behind it never needed

When the famous autographed photograph was gifted to Black Forest Inn, nobody expected this to happen. The contents in the suitcase above the bar are also rather unexpected.

BLACK FOREST INN

WHAT Never-repaired bullet holes on a world-famous photograph, plus a mysterious suitcase

WHERE Black Forest Inn, 1 E. Twenty-Sixth St., Minneapolis

COST $8 for the Black Forest torte topped with fresh whipped cream

PRO TIP Plan your meal at Black Forest Inn around a trip to the nearby Minneapolis Institute of Art. It's one of the best art museums in the country, and it's free!

repairing because, according to Erica Christ, the owner's daughter, it just happened to be bulletproof.

The bullet-riddled photo isn't the only odd thing on display. On the other side of the bar, up on a shelf, you'll see a suitcase. Inside it are a few pictures, mementos, and a jar of ashes belonging to another former patron. His name was Tony. He passed away in 2016. Throughout the last ten years of his life, Tony, an eccentric fella, sat on the stool below that shelf, drinking Grain Belt Premium and talking to almost everyone who walked through the door. He loved the community at the bar so much that he donated some of his remains to the place (the rest are in the Gulf of Mexico). Now that's some customer loyalty!

RLD'S QUIETEST PLACE

Where is there a room so quiet you might even hear your scalp crunching and arteries swooshing?

The human senses make life more meaningful. But some days, wouldn't it be nice to climb inside a room filled with nothing but deafening silence? That's what you can experience (if you can stand it) at Orfield Laboratories, the nation's only multidisciplinary sensory test lab, located in South Minneapolis. Twice now, Orfield's anechoic chamber, designed to absorb sound waves, has been declared the quietest place on earth by *Guinness World Records*. But with an unimaginable sound level of minus-thirteen decibels, it might not be as pleasant as you'd think.

Orfield Laboratories was founded by Steven Orfield nearly half a century ago. The chamber was added after he purchased the building in 1990 from his client Sound 80 Studios, the world-famous pioneering digital studio that attracted the likes of Bob Dylan, Cat Stevens, Leo Kottke, and Prince. The chamber is a thick, double-walled, insulated steel room within a room that sits in a pit, disconnected from the rest of the building. The inner chamber is covered with soundproof fiberglass wedges and echo-damping springs. "The only sound in there is you," said Orfield.

After the two doors are closed and the last of the outside noise vanishes into the walls, visitors' ears begin to adjust. The first thing they notice is the sound of their breathing. Then the thumping of their heart, the creaking of bones, the swooshing of arteries, the crunching of scalp. Some find it peaceful. Others are banging on the door to get out after a couple of minutes.

"When the ear is deprived of sound, it creates its own aural hallucinations," Orfield Laboratories owner Steven Orfield once said during a CBS news segment.

Tucked inside Orfield Laboratories—the former home of a nationally acclaimed recording studio in South Minneapolis shrouded by vines and trees—is a chamber that absorbs 99.99 percent of sound.

The purpose of the room is to test the sound pressure and frequency of products, from hospital equipment to vacuum cleaners. Orfield believes the sensory-reducing elements may also have great therapeutic potential for those suffering from post-traumatic stress disorder, autism, dementia, and other hypersensitivities.

ORFIELD LABORATORIES ANECHOIC CHAMBER

WHAT A room that has been twice declared the quietest place on earth by *Guinness World Records*

WHERE 2709 E. Twenty-Fifth St., Minneapolis

COST Group tours start at $125 per person. Payments and reservations must be made two weeks in advance.

PRO TIP The title of quietest room has since gone to a room at Microsoft's headquarters in Redmond, WA, but Orfield is determined to gain it back.

43

WINTER CARNIVAL TROVE

Tucked inside which shop basement is the largest public display of Saint Paul Winter Carnival artifacts?

Ever since a New York reporter compared Saint Paul to "another Siberia, unfit for human habitation" in 1886, the capital city has been setting the record straight. Each year, for ten days, the hardy-weathered Minnesota spirit is personified through the legendary (and weird) Saint Paul Winter Carnival.

Highlights include spectacular ice palaces, ice carving competitions, medallion hunts, parades, fireworks, mattress sledding races, and bar stool ski races, to name a few. There is also, of course, the ongoing feud between King of the Winds (Boreas) and the god of Fire (Vulcanus Rex). Boreas brings his beloved Queen of Snow and their royal court. Vulcanus Rex brings his Fire King Krewe of boisterous grown men donning capes, running suits, and goggles while riding around town on a 1932 Luverne fire truck.

Saint Paulites will tell you it's "the coolest celebration on Earth." Nowhere is the history of this frigid frolic more spectacularly preserved than inside the basement of a local antique shop situated along the Mississippi. West Saint Paul Antiques, opened in 1998 by Floyd and Linda Ruggles, is a three-story gem of memorabilia, ornate furniture, jewelry, and collections ranging from Elvis Presley to the Chicago World's Fair. At the heart of it, but in the basement, is a Saint Paul Winter Carnival Museum. A staircase lined with photographs winds to

---

Hidden in the basement of West Saint Paul Antiques is an astonishing assortment of Saint Paul Winter Carnival artifacts that spans 130 years and pays tribute to the legendary frigid frolic.

A tucked-away staircase leads to the Saint Paul Winter Carnival Museum, which includes costumed mannequins, Louis Hill's original coats for the Great Northern Railway, and over fifty showcases jam-packed with artifacts.

the lower-level treasure trove spanning 130 years.

Free and open to the public year-round, the museum features mannequins, toboggans, ice skates, and over fifty display cases of newspaper articles, buttons, medals, beer cans, miniature ice castles, capes, jackets, and gowns. The oldest artifact is a diamond pin from 1886 that's on display on a coat once worn by Louis W. Hill, son of legendary Minnesota railroad tycoon James J. Hill.

WEST SAINT PAUL ANTIQUES

WHAT Antique store with the largest public display of Saint Paul Winter Carnival artifacts

WHERE 880 Smith Ave. S., Saint Paul

COST Free

PRO TIP If you still have a little time afterward, check out the hand drum gallery across the street.

THE PERFECT GEM

Where can you ride in Minnesota's last manually operated elevator?

The Roaring Twenties was a time of prosperity, flappers, bootleggers, and jazz bands. It's also when local businesswoman Elizabeth C. Quinlan—the nation's first female clothing buyer— opened a majestic department store on Nicollet Mall.

Thanks to The 614 Company, which restored the building after saving it from demolition in the 1980s, it still stands as a landmark of old-world elegance in the heart of downtown. These days, it houses a mix of retail and office space, including JB Hudson, the oldest jewelry business in Minneapolis. Throughout the second floor, original display cases are filled with exquisite artifacts tracing the building's history.

Inspired by Elizabeth C. Quinlan's fondness of Renaissance palazzos in Florence, Italy, the five-story building features a large marble staircase with wrought-iron railings, crystal chandeliers, vaulted ceilings, and vintage Otis elevators with cage doors and manual cranks. The elevator on the right still has an operator sometimes on duty (don't expect to see any white gloves, though). It's the only manually operated elevator left in the state, a bit of trivia confirmed by The 614 Company.

In 1894, Quinlan worked at Goodfellow Dry Goods with Fred D. Young. While constantly neck and neck as top salesperson, they

YOUNG-QUINLAN BUILDING

WHAT Legendary department store with historic elevators and displays

WHERE 901 Nicollet Mall, Minneapolis

COST Free

PRO TIP The best way to experience the building's original beauty is by walking around the exterior, exploring the JB Hudson Jewelers store, and then taking one of the historic elevators up to the second floor to see the hallway displays.

The plaque on the Ninth Street and Nicollet Mall corner of the building features Quinlan's business symbol. She wanted to feature a woman of enduring beauty. But when French artist Armand-Albert Rateau unveiled a sketch of a nude woman, Quinlan thought it best if the lady was clothed. So Rateau added a string of beads around her neck.

became good friends. Young invited Quinlan to join him in a "crazy" venture of launching the first store west of the Mississippi River where women could walk in and pluck a garment right off a rack. Before that, women had to make their own outfits or hire somebody to make them. Together, they opened Fred D. Young & Company in the back of Vrooman's Glove Company at 513 Nicollet Avenue.

Quinlan eventually bought equal partnership, and the store's name was changed to the Young-Quinlan Company. Quinlan took over the business after Young died in 1911 and moved operations into what a reviewer once referred to as "one of the most beautiful store buildings in the world."

The Young-Quinlan Building has retained its classic beauty and formal elegance. Its foyer with terrazzo floors leads to three original Otis elevator cabs. The one on the far right is sometimes still operated by an attendant.

LONGFELLOW ZOO ARTIFACTS

From which zoo did a seal allegedly try to escape by leaping over Minnehaha Falls? And what's left of the zoo?

Minnehaha Regional Park has long been a serene spot to experience nature. Its majestic waterfall was memorialized by Henry Wadsworth Longfellow in his epic poem *The Song of Hiawatha*. One could never tell that for twenty-eight years, it was also home to a boisterous zoo. It goes back to 1878, when Robert Jones, a flamboyant showman who walked around town in a top hat and dress coat, opened a fish market on Hennepin Avenue.

Known to locals as "Fish," Jones was originally from the East Coast and was the first vendor to sell oysters in Minneapolis. For publicity, he'd stand outside the shop with his pet bear. Jones had so many exotic pets, in fact, that he also built a private zoo on the present site of the Basilica of St. Mary. In 1906, he moved the zoo next to Minnehaha Creek, above the falls near the current-day Minnehaha Parkway bridge that crosses over Hiawatha Avenue. He named it Longfellow Zoological Gardens.

The zoo became a bustling tourist attraction that included free-roaming flamingos, seal ponds, monkey houses, and an arena for animal shows. The remains of the zoo's beloved lion, named Hiawatha, are now stored at the Hennepin History

---

A few artifacts of the zoo, formerly located on the edge of Minnehaha Park, are still around: the Longfellow statue, the yellow Longfellow House, and the mortal remains of a beloved lion named Hiawatha.

Surrounded by prairie grass, the statue of Longfellow in a toga, now weathered and missing a hand, still remains at the site where it was dedicated in 1908. The Longfellow House is also nearby. The remains of Hiawatha the Lion are stored at the Hennepin History Museum.

Museum. According to legend, a seal once tried to escape the zoo by making its way down the creek and leaping over the falls. It was eventually caught down the Mississippi River on its way to Red Wing.

An admirer of Longfellow, Fish commissioned a statue of the poet at the zoo. He also added a yellow house that is a two-thirds-scale replica of Longfellow's home in Cambridge, Massachusetts. When Fish died in 1934, the zoo closed. The weathered Longfellow statue still stands in a field of native prairie grass. The Longfellow House, which was moved a short distance from its original location, houses a park information center and the Minnesota School of Botanical Art.

LONGFELLOW GARDENS

WHAT Remains of the exotic zoo once located on the grounds of Minnehaha Park

WHERE Longfellow Gardens in Minnehaha Park, 3933 E. Minnehaha Pkwy., Minneapolis

COST Free

PRO TIP While at Minnehaha Regional Park, stop by Sea Salt Eatery to enjoy local beer, ice cream, or oysters on the outdoor patio.

ABOVE THE REST

Where is the largest carved onyx figure in the world?

The Twin Cities area is bursting with public art treasures. The one that towers above the rest is the stirring statue inside the Saint Paul City Hall and Ramsey County Courthouse.

Made of sixty tons of porcelain white onyx, the thirty-eight-foot masterpiece features five Native Americans sitting around a fire smoking their peace pipes. From the rising smoke is a massive "god of peace." It's the crown jewel of the building's Memorial Hall, a three-story room with a mirrored ceiling and dark blue Belgian marble walls carved with the names of Ramsey County war veterans.

Originally named *God of Peace*, the statue was unveiled on May 28, 1936, and renamed *Vision of Peace* in 1994. It's a mythical translation of a Native American peace pipe ceremony that the artist, Swedish sculptor Carl Milles, witnessed a few years earlier in Ponca City, Oklahoma. Milles first created a full-size plaster model. Then, Saint Paul stone carver John Garatti and nineteen other stonecutters carved and shaped ninety-eight blocks of onyx into the final product according to Milles's plans.

The monument rotates slowly from left to right on a motorized turntable. One complete rotation takes two and a half hours. The backside includes scenes of hunting and battle. Different perspectives can also be viewed from the second and

As described by Larry Millett in his fabulous *AIA Guide to the Twin Cities*, the *Vision of Peace* sculpture draws a "hushed magic" from visitors.

The Vision of Peace, *a three-story sculpture in the Memorial Hall of the Saint Paul City Hall and Ramsey County Courthouse, is a mythical and romantic depiction of a Native American peace-pipe ceremony. It was dedicated to all war veterans of Ramsey County.*

VISION OF PEACE STATUE

WHAT A massive white onyx stone tribute to peace

WHERE Saint Paul City Hall and Ramsey County Courthouse, 15 W. Kellogg Blvd., Saint Paul

COST Free

PRO TIP Visit co.ramsey.mn.us for information on guided tours.

third floors. You can even stand right at the head. The City Hall/Courthouse, which was built during the Great Depression and underwent a $48 million renovation in the early 1990s, is an elegant time capsule of marble and bronze.

SLICE OF MEXICO

Where can you shop for homemade ceremonial dresses while filling up on authentic pupusas and tamales?

If you've got a case of the winter blues but have neither the time nor budget for a vacation, stop in at Mercado Central on East Lake Street. The edibles, music, soulful community, and handmade goods are so authentic, you're immediately transported.

Throughout the maze of shops and stalls in narrow hallways, you'll find jewelry, candy sugar skulls, purses, teddy bears, sombreros, pastries, meat, spices, charms, statues, videos on the life of Jesus, wedding dresses, First Communion dresses, Dora the Explorer backpacks, and hot cocoa mixed with warm cornmeal, chocolate, and cinnamon. At the heart of the market is the food hall abuzz with chatty Spanish-speaking locals, kitchen staff hollering out orders, and clattering trays loaded with full-on Latin flavors.

But Mercado Central is more than a place to pretend you're south of the border. It's a pillar in the community and an incubator for Hispanic and Latino entrepreneurs who have graduated from an entrepreneurial training program. In 1992, its founders—Juan Linares, Ramon Leon, and Sal Miranda— began organizing the Latino community at Sagrado Corazón Church in South Minneapolis.

The market, with support services on the upper floors, opened its doors in 1997. It provides an initial small space for start-up businesses and helps them grow into something

---

What makes this market truly special is the Latino community behind it that comes together to support entrepreneurial dreams.

With a colorful facade and filled with cultural handiwork, Mercado Central is an anchor for Lake Street revitalization. It has served as a model and breeding ground for other, now-thriving new businesses.

larger. For example, José and Noemi Payan, owners of the food stall called La Perla Tortilleria, have been so successful at the market, they now own a nearby wholesale tortilla factory.

MERCADO CENTRAL

WHAT Hispanic-themed open market and business incubator

WHERE 1515 E. Lake St., Minneapolis

COST Cultural meals, treats, trinkets, and garments for every budget

PRO TIP There's a free parking lot in the back.

CAPITOL'S UNCOVERED MOTTOES

Where were German messages uncovered beneath twenty-two layers of paint?

Designed by Cass Gilbert, the newly restored Minnesota State Capitol is one of the Midwest's most spectacular buildings. Its crowning glory is the dome, the world's second-largest self-supporting marble dome, modeled after St. Peter's Basilica in Rome. But its German-themed basement dining hall, known as the Rathskeller Cafeteria, is pretty cool too.

The idea for rathskellers originated in Germany as restaurants in town hall basements. When the Minnesota State Capitol Rathskeller opened in 1905, twenty-nine German mottoes encouraging camaraderie were painted within decorative scrolls on the walls. At the time, Germans were Minnesota's largest group of foreign-born immigrants.

Twelve years later, the designs were painted over due to pressure from alcohol prohibitionists and anti-German sentiment during World War I. In 1930, Governor Theodore Christianson ordered them restored. But over the years, the mottoes began getting painted over again.

In a 1999 project to restore the cafeteria to its original splendor, art conservator Dan Tarnoveanu of Renaissance Art, Restoration & Architecture had paint chips analyzed. It was

Capitol architect Cass Gilbert and artist Elmer E. Garnsey created the Rathskeller Cafeteria to resemble a German dining hall. Restored in 1999, it recaptures the historic setting of 1905. The motto shown here reads "Ein froher Gast ist niemals Last," which, according to a brochure from the Capitol Information Center, translates to "A cheerful guest is never a burden."

discovered that twenty-two layers of white paint had been applied over the years in the Rathskeller.

Small scalpels were used to remove the paint. Then the original designs were reproduced and stenciled onto a new layer of plaster. When possible, sections of the original artwork were kept intact. A brochure with the locations of each motto and its English translation is available in the Capitol Information Center located in Room 126.

The restoration of the Capitol's Rathskeller Cafeteria was the culmination of ten years of research, design, construction, and using small scalpels to remove lots of old paint.

ARK OF LIFE

Where can you get spooked in a Frankenstein laboratory, and what does it have to do with the creation of the pacemaker?

In 1931, a curious little boy named Earl Bakken went to see the film *Frankenstein*. While in the dark theater watching a mad scientist restore a corpse, he became fascinated by the potential of electricity being the difference between life and death. He watched the film over and over. One day, this prodigy, who was educated in the Columbia Heights Public Schools and at the University of Minnesota, would grow up and become cofounder of Medtronic—the world's leading medical technology company—which started in his garage.

On Halloween of 1957, a Minneapolis power outage caused the death of a baby dependent on a bulky, tabletop plug-in pacemaker. In response, Dr. C. Walton Lillehei asked Bakken, a humble electrical engineer at the time, to devise a battery-powered pacemaker small enough to tape to a patient's chest. It was a major turning point in medicine. Soon after, Medtronic began work on implantable pacemakers. At one point, Bakken—who died of natural causes at age ninety-four on October 21, 2018—became a beneficiary of his own invention.

"What intrigued me the most, as I sat through the movie again and again," Bakken said, "was the creative spark of Dr. Frankenstein's electricity. Through the power of his wildly flashing laboratory apparatus, the doctor restored life to the unliving." (Source: *Medcity News*, October 31, 2014.)

The Bakken Museum,
in 1928 by architect (
was originally a home
Goodfellow, a merchc
dry goods store to the

THE BAKKEN MUSEUM

WHAT Ongoing Frankenstein exhibit

WHERE 3537 Zenith Ave. S., Minneapolis

COST Admission, $5–$10

PRO TIP Before you go, check the museum website at thebakken.org for any updates as a result of the renovation.

In 1975, Bakken also founded The Bakken Museum. Tucked away in a mansion surrounded by gardens, it's a one-of-a-kind journey through the mysteries of electricity and magnetism. Within this treasure is the spooky Frankenstein's Laboratory. While the story of Frankenstein's monster is narrated, lights dim and flicker, thunder claps, and glaring red eyes stare through a window above a covered "corpse."

In January 2020, the museum began a six-month renovation in its lower-level wing near Bde Maka Ska. The long-term plan includes more interactive exhibits, modernized classroom space, improved accessibility, expanded programming, and a dramatic new entrance. The West Winds Mansion portion of the museum, along with the Frankenstein Laboratory, will remain open on weekends throughout the project.

WHERE THE WATERS MEET

Which spot is thought to be the center of the earth by many Dakota people?

The place where the Mississippi and Minnesota rivers come together, located within Fort Snelling State Park (and below Fort Snelling), is itself a complex story. To European settlers, it was the center of trade and military authority. But to many Dakota people, who call it Bdote, it's the center of the earth. As Gwen Westerman and Bruce White wrote in their book *Mni Sota Makoce: The Land of the Dakota*, "It's where the Dakota people came from the stars to be on the earth."

But that location is also where some of their people suffered and died. In the wake of the US–Dakota War of 1862, sixteen hundred Dakota noncombatants (many of them women and children) were marched more than 150 miles to that area, where they were confined. At least 130 died during the cold winter months of captivity. Survivors were deported to Crow Creek in southeastern South Dakota and later to a reservation in Nebraska. There's a powerful memorial near the entrance to the Pike Island trail.

This sacred confluence can be accessed from the three-mile loop around Pike Island, one of the Twin Cities' best urban hikes. Enter through Fort Snelling State Park, where you'll need to pay a fee unless you have a state park sticker. Or you can park at Fort

"The confluence area of the Mississippi and Minnesota rivers is known to many Dakota as Bdote—or the place of creation. As such, it is also considered the center of Dakota spirituality and history." (Source: USDakotawar.org.)

The confluence of the Mississippi and Minnesota rivers is located almost directly between Minneapolis and Saint Paul. A memorial to the Dakota people stands near the entrance to the Pike Island trail.

Snelling with no charge and follow the path down the hill. Veer right and then follow the Pike Island sign to the footbridge over the Minnesota River. As you cross the bridge there's a trail that branches off to the right, which heads to the Minnesota River side of the island. To the left is the trail to the Mississippi River side.

CONFLUENCE OF MINNESOTA AND MISSISSIPPI RIVERS

WHAT Sacred place of creation to the Dakota people

WHERE Pike Island, Fort Snelling State Park, 101 Snelling Lake Rd., Saint Paul

COST Free

PRO TIP A Bdote Memory Map at bdotememorymap.org allows you to listen to Dakota voices as you experience the site. Also, the Minnesota Humanities Center offers a tour called "Learning from Place: Bdote," which features sites along the Mississippi River that are significant to the Dakota.

HEAVENLY COOKIES

Where is there a cookie shop opened by a nun who used to walk around town telling stories with a stuffed monkey?

While working as a teacher and adult religious educator at Our Lady of Grace Church in Edina, the late Sister Jean Thuerauf could often be seen on weekends walking the streets of North Minneapolis. She'd tell kids stories with Jocko, her stuffed monkey. Then in 1976, after nearly dying from a brain virus, she felt called to live in North Minneapolis.

With a heart for youth vulnerable to crime, violence, and gang activity, she began inviting children and teenagers into her tiny kitchen to provide homework help. In turn, they'd help her bake cookies. She'd give the kids jobs peddling cookies on the sidewalk, using a cart the kids helped paint. Before long, there were more bakers than there was room. But Sister Jean had an idea.

In 1988, her vision for a safe and engaging space for North Minneapolis youth formalized and was registered as a nonprofit bakery called Cookie Cart. Sister Jean died at the age of eighty-five in 2016 at Catholic Elder Care, but her legacy lives on. The lives of more than ten thousand kids have been touched through Cookie Cart.

Today, the shop brings in more than $500,000 a year in sales of cookies and employs some three hundred teenagers.

COOKIE CART

WHAT A nonprofit bakery launched by a nun in 1988 that provides a safe haven for youth living in low-income communities to learn life skills

WHERE 1119 W. Broadway Ave., Minneapolis; 946 Payne Ave., Saint Paul

COST $1 per cookie

PRO TIP Sister Jean also authored two books: *Echoes from the City*, published in 1977, and *Deprived of Dignity*, published in 1996.

Cookie Cart is a nonprofit bakery in North Minneapolis and now also the Payne-Phalen neighborhood of Saint Paul. It gives youth living in low-income communities the opportunity for a job and to learn life skills.

THIS BUILDING IS DEDICATED TO

SISTER JEAN THUERAUF

VISIONARY AND FOUNDER OF COOKIE CART

SEPTEMBER 8, 1930 · JUNE 6, 2016

All proceeds go toward running the shop and paying the employees, who work hard to learn work, life, and leadership skills. A second Cookie Cart is now open in the Payne-Phalen neighborhood of Saint Paul. There are ten different types of cookies that can be purchased as singles or by the box for events.

Known as "The Mother Teresa of the Northside," Sister Jean Thuerauf opened Cookie Cart in 1988 after teenagers began lining up on her porch for homework help and to bake cookies with her.

How did a ping-pong ball inspire a puppetry legacy?

We're all born with a primal instinct for wonder and imagination. But sometimes those muscles need exercise. Introducing Z Puppets Rosenschnoz! By mixing handcrafted puppetry, zany comedy, and live music into mindful entertainment for all ages, the Minneapolis-based nonprofit has been tapping into the imaginations of audience members across the country for more than twenty years. And to think it all started with a ping-pong ball.

Playwright Shari Aronson and street performer Chris Griffith met at the In the Heart of the Beast Puppet and Mask Theatre, the Twin Cities' gateway for puppetry. One day in 1998, they made a discovery that changed the course of their lives. For whatever reason, the curious duo shined a blacklight onto a ping-pong ball. Lo and behold, the ball glowed in the dark.

Aronson and Griffith were both so enchanted that they started a circus-tent puppet booth featuring a whole pack of ping-pong balls, which they painted with fluorescent paint. Before long, that endeavor grew into a full-blown, glow-in-the-dark, ping-pong ball circus featuring tightrope walkers, clowns, daredevils, and ping-pong performers. They named it the Amazing Gnip Gnop Circus.

Since then, Z Puppets Rosenschnoz has brought over twenty-five original puppetry productions and "gazillions" of workshops to schools, theaters, libraries, festivals, and summer camps. They're perhaps best known for the show

---

"As performers, we delight in giving inanimate objects the illusion of life." (Source: Z Puppets Rosenschnoz website.)

You'd never guess how extraordinary Z Puppets is by its humble homebase with the green door on Chicago Avenue. The puppet shown here is Mr. Punch. He's featured in The Comical Misadventures of Mr. Punch, one of the company's twenty-five original puppetry productions.

Monkey Mind Pirates, designed to give kids creative tools to overcome anxiety, stress, and distraction. There is also a *Monkey Mind Pirates* CD that comes with instructions for creating your own monkey shadow puppet.

Although rich with playfulness, many of their shows cover profound topics of struggle, loss, and triumph. *Through the Narrows*, for example, features a thirty-five-thousand-year-old Jewish woman who was with Moses at the crossing of the Red Sea and a six-year-old Cherokee time traveler bearing witness to the Trail of Tears.

Z PUPPETS ROSENSCHNOZ

WHAT Performing arts troupe

WHERE 4054 Chicago Ave. S., Minneapolis (with events and workshops throughout the metro)

COST $10–$25

PRO TIP Check zpuppets.org for events calendar.

LARGEST LITE-BRITE

How many pegs are in the world's largest Lite-Brite? And where is it?

Union Depot in Lowertown is one of America's great transportation hubs. As you enter from Fourth Street and walk through the dazzling entryway, you feel the historic splendor: pink marbled floors, tall symmetrical columns, arched steel windows, and vaulted ceilings with Guastavino tile. The last thing you expect to see is a Guinness World Record Lite-Brite mounted to the wall.

The Lite-Brite was created in 2013 to launch an unprecedented challenge called "Forever Saint Paul." The challenge attracted nearly a thousand ideas from Minnesotans who answered the question: What would you do with $1 million to make Saint Paul great? To kick off the search for the best and "brightest" ideas, six hundred community members volunteered more than eight hundred hours to hand sort 596,897 teeny tiny plastic pegs by color. Then they assembled the pegs into a mural design created by local artist Ta-coumba Aiken.

Fondly known as "The Mayor of Lowertown," Aiken is the force behind some of Minnesota's most acclaimed public artworks, including the Jax/Gillette Children's Hospital mural, the tile around the fourth-floor fireplace at the Minneapolis Central Library, the concrete relief figures decorating the entrance to the Seventh and Robert Street Municipal Parking Ramp, and the mural on the grain elevator in Good Thunder, Minnesota.

The Union Depot was originally completed in 1926 and fully restored in 2011–2012. The twelve-foot-by-twenty-foot Lite-Brite in the waiting room is lit up with energy-efficient, long-lasting LEDs.

Permanently installed at the Union Depot, the Lite-Brite project was led by local artist Ta-coumba Aiken, whose tagline is "I create my art to heal the hearts and souls of people and their communities by evoking a positive spirit."

At its peak, the neoclassical depot station served as many as twenty thousand travelers a day, including US presidents, international royalty, and movie stars. Now fully restored after a four-decade absence of passenger trains and a massive renovation project completed in 2012, it's the train station of the Twin Cities and part of the Amtrak national passenger train system. It also serves as a hub for community events including concerts, yoga nights, and Bloody Mary festivals.

WILD THING

What's the inspiration behind a bookstore with a furry black chicken and cats without tails on the loose?

Wild Rumpus, a children's bookstore nestled in the quaint village of Linden Hills, might be the most magical retail space on the planet. Its miniature purple doorway out front has been luring kids and their parents for more than a quarter of a century.

The creaky-floored treasure trove houses approximately thirty-six thousand titles in twenty languages. The scariest ones are secluded inside a "haunted hut." The store takes its name from Maurice Sendak's 1963 book *Where the Wild Things Are.* But the interior design is based on Anne Mazer's 1991 book *The Salamander Room,* in which a boy's bedroom is gradually transformed into the outdoors.

WILD RUMPUS BOOKSTORE

WHAT A literary haven that lets its wild side run loose—literally

WHERE 2720 W. Forty-Third St., Minneapolis

COST Various prices for young reader books and classics for adults

PRO TIP Sebastian Joe's ice cream shop is a block away, and so is Heartfelt, a lovely toy shop where kids can drop in and make a wooden craft.

To turn their wild dreams into reality, cofounders Collette Morgan and the late Tom Braun worked with an architect of a tree house they had long admired. Progressing through the store is like wandering into the portal of an enchanted forest.

The children's bookstore even has a pet-store license so Minneapolis officials can inspect and ensure the safety and well-being of the animals.

A magical place to experience the rich literary culture of the Twin Cities is through the little purple door to Wild Rumpus. In 2017, it became the first children's bookstore to be named Publishers Weekly *Bookstore of the Year.*

A shy Japanese Silkie bantam chicken named Neil DeGrasse Tyson silently brushes past your leg. Cats without tails named Booker T and Eartha Kitt, whose breed originated from an islet in the middle of the northern Irish Sea, climb on top of the cash register. Ferrets, lizards, chinchillas, doves, and a tarantula named Hagrid scamper in caged enclosures. Aquarium fish stare at you while you wash your hands in the bathroom. And the store's ceiling appears to crack open to the sky as an upside down birch canoe hangs from it (see photo in center insert) while a tree trimmer climbs a ladder into the sheetrock. It's truly a walk on the wild side.

MR. JIMMY'S BENCH

What does a little wooden bench on the main drag of Excelsior have to do with the Rolling Stones?

As a popular Twin Cities summer destination, the quaint town of Excelsior on the shores of Lake Minnetonka offers everything you'd ever want: beach, band shell, boutiques, breweries, and an ice cream shop with banana splits from heaven. It even has a street corner bench you can rest your bum upon and become part of rock-and-roll history.

Marked by a small plaque, the bench pays tribute to the late James Lee Hutmaker, who moved to Excelsior at age sixteen in 1948. He became a town ambassador of sorts. Nicknamed Mr. Jimmy, he was engaging and intelligent, despite some quirky traits. It's been reported that he was deeply affected by a childhood tragedy. He witnessed his nanny fatally engulfed in flames when she lit the family's stove. For decades, while living at his brother's house (182 Third Street, now a registered historic site), he roamed the streets dressed in disheveled layers of vintage clothing, chewing an unlit cigar, carrying a briefcase, and learning everybody's name. According to legend, he also inspired a Rolling Stones song.

One night in 1964, the Stones performed at the former Excelsior Amusement Park. The next day Mick Jagger went to the local drugstore, then named Bacon Drug, to pick up a prescription. Hutmaker happened to be ordering a Cherry Coke at the soda fountain. When Hutmaker received a regular Coke

---

Hutmaker, who passed away at the age of seventy-five in 2007, relished his encounters with people on the streets. "I like people. You don't feel alone when you have friends," he once said. (Source: *Southwest News Media*.)

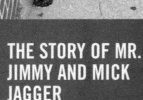

His part in Rolling Stones lore is just one aspect of Mr. Jimmy's legacy. One night he showed up at the town's annual Christmas pageant wearing the tuxedo his good friend Bob Bolles had given to him and stunned the crowd by singing a beautiful rendition of "White Christmas." Photo of Mr. Jimmy courtesy of Bob Bolles.

THE STORY OF MR. JIMMY AND MICK JAGGER

WHAT A bench that memorializes a beloved resident who became part of Rolling Stones lore

WHERE Northwest corner of Water and Lake streets, Excelsior

COST Free

PRO TIP While in town, check out gems like Excelsior Bay Books and Leipold's. Or walk down to the docks and treat yourself to an award-winning hot dog from Tommy's Tonka Trolley.

instead, he turned and said to Jagger, "You can't always get what you want."

Five years later, the Stones released their massive hit titled "You Can't Always Get What You Want." The song includes references to a drugstore, cherry red, a prescription, and Mr. Jimmy. Jagger has never verified the connection. But recorded accounts by Mr. Jimmy's friends and relatives and also the waitress who served the regular Coke to Jimmy that night suggest the encounter is true.

LIVESTOCK UNIVERSE

Which quiet Twin Cities community used to be home to the world's largest stockyards?

South Saint Paul is an overlooked treasure. It not only has a lovely renewed riverfront but also smells like freshly baked bagels thanks to Twin City Bagel's headquarters. One could never tell that for more than a century, the community was home to one of the largest, stinkiest livestock centers in the universe.

That's all gone, though, except for a few remnants. One of them is a pair of brick entrance gates still at the site of the now-demolished Armour meatpacking plant. Another is the former Union Stockyards Company Exchange Building, a majestic structure that now houses a special events center.

Around 1885, Alpheus Beede Stickney, president of the Chicago Great Western Railway, bought land along the Mississippi River to establish the South Saint Paul stockyards. Then, two Chicago meatpacking companies—Swift in 1897 and Armour in 1919—opened plants next door. Trainloads of cattle and hogs rolled in day and night. They were turned into beef, pork, leather, lard, medicine, fertilizer, even Dial soap.

Thousands of people, including immigrants from Serbia, Croatia, Romania, Poland, and other European countries, worked at the plants, according to writings by local historian Lois Glewwe. They lived in temporary boarding houses on Concord Street. In the midst of rancid odors, they made the best of it and performed their grisly tasks well. After hours they'd unwind together at the

"Today in South Saint Paul, the stockyard is gone, Swift is gone, Armour is gone. But a legacy remains—the Twin Cities they helped build, filled with people who love burgers and bacon."
(Source: *Pioneer Press*, November 13, 2015.)

The beautiful Exchange Building, reflected here in the building across from it, was built in 1887 as the base of operations for the stockyards. Another memento is the red brick gate posts of the former Armour meatpacking giant.

surplus of local dives like Hook-Em Cow Café.

Work at the plants was disrupted by regular floods and strikes. Eventually, due to changing market forces, Swift closed in 1969. Ten years later, the Armour plant closed. Both closings led to disastrous unemployment levels. South Saint Paul charted a new course, though, including an expensive clean-up, a pristine riverfront park, a trail system, and better-smelling businesses.

SOUTH SAINT PAUL STOCKYARDS

WHAT The few visible signs remaining of a global livestock legacy

WHERE The Exchange Building, 200 Concord St. N.; Armour gates, 325 Armour Ave., South Saint Paul

COST Free

PRO TIP South Saint Paul is loaded with gems, such as the Commemorative Air Force Minnesota Wing Museum, where you can take a history flight on authentic WWII aircraft.

FALLS FIASCO

How did a tunnel built below St. Anthony Falls nearly ruin Minneapolis?

St. Anthony Falls is historically one of Minneapolis's most important places. Its fifty-foot drop into the Mississippi River provided extraordinary power for the milling industries that transformed Minneapolis into "The Milling Capital of the World." But all that was nearly destroyed when the falls came close to collapsing after two businessmen built a twenty-five-hundred-foot tunnel below the riverbed.

In the 1860s, the St. Anthony Mill Company and the Minneapolis Mill Company monopolized the river's water power. But that monopoly was challenged in a heated battle in 1865 when William W. Eastman and John L. Merriam bought a large portion of Nicollet Island, located in the middle of the river near Minneapolis. Eventually, Eastman and Merriam were allowed to create a tailrace tunnel that ran under the Mississippi River to the tip of Nicollet Island. But it would turn into one of the greatest environmental catastrophes Minneapolis had ever seen.

The online Historyapolis Project describes the fiasco: "In 1869, the tunnel collapsed and the river flooded in, creating a massive underground vortex. Over the next six years, recurring collapses turned the riverfront into a series of sinkholes and whirlpools that swallowed multiple mills. Minneapolis and St. Anthony both faced economic ruin . . . If left unchecked, the

St. Anthony Falls is known as the birthplace of Minneapolis for the power it provided for milling industries. But all that came close to ruin when two enterprising fellows tried to build a tunnel underneath the river to Nicollet Island.

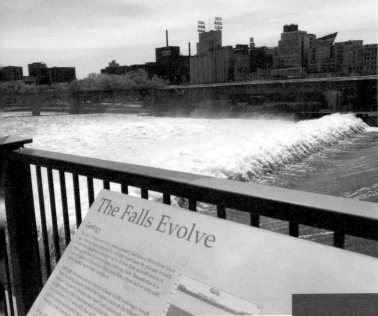

This photo was taken from Water Power Park, owned by Xcel Energy but open to the public. It's easily accessed from historic St. Anthony Main and is a great place to read interpretive signs while taking in views of the Riverfront District.

tunnel disaster could destroy the falls and permanently cripple urban development along the river corridor. Without a waterfall to build on, Minneapolis would lose its reason to exist."

Eventually, the US Army Corps of Engineers intervened by constructing a dam underneath the river bed. The falls were finally stabilized with a concrete overflow spillway. Eastman eventually succeeded in bringing water power to Nicollet Island in 1879 by using an overland power cable. Part of the island is now a cobblestoned, residential gem (read more in "Neon-Lit Island," page 26).

ST. ANTHONY FALLS AND THE EASTMAN TUNNEL FIASCO

WHAT A tunnel collapse below the river at St. Anthony Falls nearly turned Minneapolis into a sinkhole.

WHERE Feel the power of the falls at the St. Anthony Falls Lock and Dam Visitor Center, 1 Portland Ave., or Water Power Park, 204 Main St. SE, Minneapolis.

COST Free

PRO TIP Leave time to walk through Mill Ruins Park near the Visitor Center. Other great spots to view the falls include the Endless Bridge at the Guthrie Theater and the observation deck at Mill City Museum (which requires a super cool elevator ride to get to it).

WHITE CASTLE #8

Where is there a portable White Castle that sells lovely home goods but no sliders?

The craving for those little square burgers steamed atop a pile of onions (a.k.a. gut bombs) can get pretty intense for some. But you're out of luck if you stumble upon the White Castle building on the corner of Thirty-Third Street and Lyndale Avenue in South Minneapolis hoping to satisfy your cravings with a sack of those succulent sliders. Why? Because the eighth White Castle to open in Minneapolis is now operated as an antique/vintage goods shop called Xcentric Goods.

Constructed in 1936, its exterior is classic White Castle, with the porcelain enamel, turrets, and towers fit for a princess designed after the Chicago Water Tower. It's one of only a few White Castle buildings of this type left in the country. Despite the "Buy 'em by the sack" slogan still on the storefront, what you'll find inside is a hodgepodge of antique furnishings, fine art, jewelry, and lighting. If you're "lucky," you might even find a slider-scented candle in the mix.

Built to be dismantled and moved, this is the third location for White Castle #8. It started off at 616 Washington Avenue. In 1950, when the owner of the property refused to renew the lease, it was moved to 329 Central Avenue. In 1983, it faced demolition because a bigger White Castle opened down the road.

Landowners were often reluctant to extend leases on the small hamburger shops. So White Castle constructed some of its buildings to be easily moved. White Castle #8 on Lyndale Avenue, now an antique shop, has had three locations.

Fifty-five of these portable castles were manufactured between 1928 and 1942. White Castle #8 in Minneapolis, a twenty-eight-by-twenty-eight-foot cultural artifact, is one of the few that remain.

Fortunately, it received a spot on the National Register of Historic Places. When a new buyer relocated the building to its current location, it was decommissioned as a restaurant. Prior to its current tenant, it housed a contracting firm and then an accordion repair and jewelry business. The Xcentric Goods sign isn't allowed to be attached because of the building's historic stature.

PORTABLE WHITE CASTLE

WHAT The eighth White Castle to open in Minneapolis turned into a vintage home goods store

WHERE Xcentric Goods, 3252 Lyndale Ave. S., Minneapolis

COST Something for every budget

PRO TIP Open Thursday through Sunday. If you absolutely must have a slider and some onion rings, there's a real White Castle less than a mile away at 100 West Lake Street.

REALLY BIG SNOWMAN

Where is there a giant snowman that hasn't melted in fifty years?

Given the average annual snowfall, it's not all that surprising to learn that Minnesota is home to "the world's largest snowman." But when you see that snowman while driving along Highway 36 in the middle of July, it can rattle you a little. Made out of stucco and chicken wire, the unofficial mascot of North Saint Paul stands forty feet tall, weighs twenty tons, and boasts a smile that's sixteen feet long. It even has a cute little door on its behind for maintenance workers.

In 1969, Lloyd Koesling, a civic leader and resident of North Saint Paul, wanted to create a welcoming symbol to represent his town. He felt a snowman was a good fit. Each year, the North Saint Paul Jaycees built a big snowman as part of the annual snow festival, using the excess snow the plowing crew would drop off. But even in Minnesota, the snow is a little lean some winters.

The Chamber of Commerce agreed to finance Koesling's idea for a permanent snowman. In 1972, volunteers came together to begin pouring the foundation and welding rods into arms and three balls. The smallest of the balls was hoisted on top by a crane. Then one thousand pounds of stucco was added to the structure. The whole project took more than two years and cost about two thousand dollars.

With few exits leading to North Saint Paul, it's often referred to as "the town the freeway forgot." But a great big smiley snowman next to Highway 36 attempts to lure you in.

The snowman was built in the early 1970s and designed by a local civic leader who wished to create a lasting image for his town. There are other snowman structures bigger than this one now, but it's reported to still be the largest stucco snowman.

NORTH SAINT PAUL'S SNOWY MASCOT

WHAT A giant stucco snowman that tries to entice you to visit a wonderful but overlooked town

WHERE 2601 Centennial Dr., North Saint Paul

COST Free

PRO TIP North Saint Paul is dotted with beaches, parks, and mom-and-pop shops. Check out the pair of bullfrogs kept in an aquarium in the front window of the legendary Neumann's Bar & Grill.

For nearly twenty years, the snowman stood on North Saint Paul's main street. Because the quiet, old-style small town often gets overlooked, the decision was made in 1990 to move the snowman to the current location on the corner of Margaret Street and Highway 36 to catch the attention of passersby. Spiffed up in 2017 with a fresh coat of paint, the snowman stands today in its frosty glory as a warm, hearty welcome to both travelers and locals.

"SUPER-SECRET" SPEAKEASY

Where do food servers appear through secret mirrors?

There's no sign. No main street entrance. No phone. No social media accounts. Only a one-page website with nothing but an email link for reservations. Even so, lots of informed and determined people (and Google Maps users, but that only partially helps) manage to find their way to Volstead's Emporium, hidden in a back alley in Minneapolis's Lyn-Lake area.

The "secret" Prohibition-themed haunt is named after US Representative Andrew Volstead. Volstead is the Minnesotan who wrote the Eighteenth Amendment banning alcohol in the United States from 1920 to 1933, causing cocktailing to move to the underground in the form of speakeasies.

If you stop someone on the street to ask for directions, insiders might give clues like "Hang a left at the first alley, and keep going past the dumpsters until you see a red light." Once you're in front of the creepy, bolted backdoor entrance, knock. When a bouncer slides open the peephole, smile, say hi, and let him know if you have reservations or not. He may or may not ask for a password. If he does, just make one up. Then wait for him to kindly let you in and descend into the candle-lit basement.

From red velvet curtains, chandeliers, and hidden doors to the cozy fire, dim lighting, and smooth jazz music, you'll feel like you're in a time warp to the Roaring Twenties. In the booths

---

Finding the secret entrance to Volstead's Emporium is half the fun. Once you do, it's a magical experience that includes food servers popping out through mirrors and hidden doors leading to secret rooms.

Volstead's is very committed to the speakeasy theme. At night, a red light above this creepy, bolted door lets you know you've found the right place. Once inside, look for the portrait of US Representative Andrew Volstead, the Minnesotan who wrote the Eighteenth Amendment banning alcohol in the United States from 1920 to 1933.

along the wall, servers appear through mirrors that open inward (so drinks can be quickly dumped "in a police raid"). Dave West, a digital designer, and John Braun, a real estate lawyer, opened Volstead's in 2015 after first planning it out on a napkin. The menu includes inventive craft cocktails and small, delicious plates that change with the seasons.

VOLSTEAD'S EMPORIUM

WHAT A speakeasy named after the Minnesotan who penned the National Prohibition Act

WHERE Hidden in a creepy alley in the Lyn-Lake neighborhood, Minneapolis

COST Food items and cocktails medium to pricey

PRO TIP Avoid waiting outside in the cold alley for a table by going right when it opens at 5 p.m. or by emailing reservations@volsteads.com. Try to get a booth if you can.

NOMADIC TREASURES

Where can you stand inside an authentic camel-herding hut?

With blizzards and biting winds directly from the North Pole, Minnesota seems the least likely place for African refugees. Yet tens of thousands of people born in Somalia and of Somali descent have made it their home since civil war broke out in their country in 1991.

The strength of local agencies has helped them find housing, get health care, learn English, and begin a new life. In the Twin Cities, members of the Somali community can also reconnect with their roots at the Somali Museum of Minnesota. Consisting of five rooms tucked in the basement of a storefront on East Lake Street, it's been touted as the only museum dedicated to the Somali culture anywhere in the world.

A national gallery once existed in Mogadishu, the capital of Somalia. But years of war led to its destruction. Featured throughout the gallery are over seven hundred artifacts and signage describing the violence that drove the refugees to Minnesota. In the biggest room is a full-size Somali hut, the kind used by nomadic camel-herding people in rural Somalia. Some of the artifacts were donated by families and artists in Somalia. But most have been collected by the museum's founder, Osman Mohamed Ali.

The largest Somali diaspora community in the United States lives in Minnesota. The Somali Museum in Minneapolis shares the East African story with people of all backgrounds while helping young Somalis catch hold of their traditional culture before it disappears.

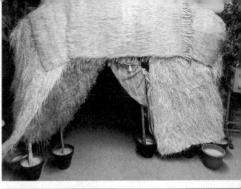

Featured throughout the gallery are hundreds of cultural artifacts, including a life-size camel-herding hut, contemporary paintings, milk and water vessels, and beautiful woven goods designed by Somali women.

SOMALI MUSEUM OF MINNESOTA

WHAT World's only Somali museum

WHERE 1516 E. Lake St., Minneapolis (They are looking for a bigger space, so check their website for any updates before you go.)

COST Admission, $8–$11

PRO TIP Minneapolis is also home to Karmel Mall, the nation's first Somali mall, located at 2944 Pillsbury Ave. South.

Ali, a father of eight and a local restaurant owner, has traveled throughout Somalia to collect objects and treasures from nomadic communities. The museum offers an unrivaled opportunity for people of all backgrounds to learn about East African culture. It also features outreach programs, including a traveling dance troupe and a mobile culture show, that are available to visit schools or other organizations.

TRACES OF TROLLEYS

What's left of those charming yellow streetcars that used to fill the Twin Cities' streets?

Nothing stirs up nostalgia for days gone by more than the *clang clang clang* and the *ding ding ding* of an electric streetcar (a.k.a trolley). In the late nineteenth century and the first half of the twentieth century, they crisscrossed nearly every Twin Cities neighborhood from Stillwater to Excelsior. At its peak in 1920, when the fare was six cents, the Twin Cities Rapid Transit Company (TCRT) reported carrying a record 238 million passengers. By then the infrastructure had grown to include nine hundred cars.

It all started coming to a screeching halt in 1952, though, when automobiles began to be more affordable. Deemed impractical and unreliable, the majority of those streetcars were burned and the rails ripped out or paved over. But a few artifacts remain, including eight historic streetcars maintained through the Minnesota Streetcar Museum. Six of them are available for rides on demonstration railways in Minneapolis and Excelsior.

A lesser-known artifact is the sealed up Selby Avenue Trolley Tunnel. Covered in graffiti, the lower east entrance is still visible down the slope from the

---

MINNESOTA STREETCAR MUSEUM LINE AND SELBY AVENUE TUNNEL

WHAT Remaining remnants of the Twin Cities' good old trolley days

WHERE Selby Tunnel entrance down the slope from the Cathedral of Saint Paul; historic trolley ride locations at trolleyride.org

COST Single trolley ride, $2.50; family season pass, $60

PRO TIP There used to be streetcar boats too. They were purposely sunk when deemed no longer financially viable. One of them was raised up and restored after lying on the bottom of Lake Minnetonka for fifty years. Go to steamboatminnehaha.org for a schedule and tickets.

The upper portal of the Selby Avenue Tunnel and the deep trench leading to it in the middle of Selby Avenue were filled in and paved over. But the lower east portal is still visible down the slope from the cathedral. A rugged pathway and an information sign lead you to it.

Cathedral of Saint Paul. You'll find it tucked back off the pathway, sometimes nearly hidden by overgrown grass and trees.

The Selby-Lake line that passed through the Selby Tunnel was one of the most popular routes in the entire streetcar system. Near the end of the route was the St. Anthony Hill. It proved too steep for the electric streetcars to climb. In 1907, TCRT dug a 1,472-foot-long, two-track tunnel under Selby Avenue to an opening near Nina Street, cutting the grade in half. When the streetcar system was dismantled, however, the two entrances to the tunnel were sealed.

To make it possible for electric cars to climb and descend the Selby Hill without cable assistance, the Selby Avenue Trolley Tunnel was built to cut the grade in half.

PLAYGROUND MUSEUM

Where can you shout through, sit on, and run around weird and renowned sculptures a half mile from the State Capitol?

While driving along Marion Street, just west of the Capitol, you'll pass by a playground tucked between two rows of apartment buildings in a densely populated neighborhood. But you'll quickly notice this is no ordinary playground. It's like a playground museum featuring a rotating collection of about fifteen large-scale, fantastical sculptures by local, national, and international artists.

Public Art Saint Paul (PASP) is the organization that has curated and maintained the sculptures in this diverse neighborhood since 1998. According to its website, the whimsical park, known as Western Sculpture Park, has been "a transformational force that has improved neighborhood conditions overall."

The first thing to grab your attention is the swirling, bright red, steel cylinder sculpture by Alexander Liberman. Titled *Above, Above*, it was donated by Ecolab in 2017. A new sculpture that joined the park is a playful aardvark that also doubles as a storage shed.

Other structures include a big yellow megaphone called *Democracy Speaks* that you can yell or yodel through and a

---

If you're addicted to sculptures, the Twin Cities area is the place for you. Although it's in plain sight, the Western Sculpture Park, featuring large-scale, whimsical sculptures, gets overlooked in favor of more distinguished sculpture parks and museums.

If you're driving along Marion Street, Western Sculpture Park comes as quite a surprise. Since 1997, Public Art Saint Paul, in partnership with Saint Paul Parks & Recreation and Franconia Sculpture Park, has produced a sculpture exhibition, education programs, and cultural events there.

thirty-three-foot steel sculpture called *Walking Warrior* by Melvin Smith that stands in honor of civil rights protest marchers. Internationally acclaimed sculptor Mark di Suvero contributed *Grace à Toi*, which features four towering steel beams supporting a metal globe of sorts that moves when the wind blows. There are also a couple of lovely benches to sit on, such as the one attached to a friendly skull with red protruding lips.

WESTERN SCULPTURE PARK

WHAT A curated sculpture exhibition where you least expect it

WHERE 387 Marion St., Saint Paul

COST Free

PRO TIP From the park, you can see the Minnesota State Capitol, the Cathedral of Saint Paul, and the Minnesota History Center.

BLIND IS BEAUTY

How did a historic Pillsbury mansion become a modern-day center for the blind? And what's the story behind the fireplace in the executive director's office?

It's been proven time and time again that blind people can live full and amazing lives. And there's no better place to learn how to do so than at BLIND Inc. (BLIND stands for Blindness: Learning in New Dimensions), located in a castle-style mansion in South Minneapolis. The mansion was originally built by local flour-milling legend Charles Stinson Pillsbury, the son of local flour-milling legend Charles Alfred Pillsbury.

The center, founded in 1986 by the National Federation of the Blind (NFB), started out in a two-bedroom apartment. But Joyce Scanlan, its visionary executive director during the formative years, dreamed of housing classes and activities in a great big, lovely old home.

When the Pillsbury English Gothic mansion became available in 1994, Scanlan leaped over whatever hurdles stood in her way. Now a nationally acclaimed rehabilitation center that has kept the mansion's historical character intact, BLIND draws in people of all ages from Minnesota and other states to participate in its preemployment, empowerment, and independent living programs. Graduates of its full-time program receive a freedom bell to celebrate their new independence.

BLIND, INCORPORATED

WHAT A center for the blind located in a former Pillsbury mansion

WHERE 100 Twenty-Second St. E., Minneapolis

COST Free tours by appointment

PRO TIP Down the block is Washburn Fair Oaks Park, across from the Minneapolis Institute of Art. Take a few minutes to read the information sign about the elaborate Washburn mansion that once stood there.

Although the mansion looks like a Renaissance estate from the outside, it was actually built like a modern skyscraper, with I-beam construction and wood placed over concrete floors, which is why it has lasted so long. The story of the fireplace in the executive director's office is also rather unexpected.

The building's history is filled with intriguing stories. One of them involves the fireplace in the executive director's office. Featuring a small sculpture of angels taking the head of John the Baptist to heaven, it survived the Great Fire of London in 1666. After that, the fireplace was purchased by William Randolph Hearst, known for developing Hearst Communications, the nation's largest newspaper chain and media company. Charles S. Pillsbury, an acquaintance of Hearst, liked the fireplace so much that he asked for an exact copy to be made for him.

On its voyage to the United States from overseas, the box with the original fireplace got switched with the box of the replica. Therefore, the Pillsbury family ended up receiving the original in their mansion. It's still there today, despite years of lawsuits by Hearst, who eventually gave up trying to get it back.

The uniqueness of the former Pillsbury mansion, which now houses a school for the blind, includes some surprisingly modern architectural features and an intriguing history.

MARQUETTE PLAZA (page 112)

SKYROCK FARM AND CAROUSEL (page 154)

Full color insert photos courtesy of Debra Bernard Photography.

MIDWAY MURALS (page 192)

WILD RUMPUS BOOKSTORE (page 66)

SWEDE HOLLOW (page 18)

HAMM'S BREWERY (page 124)

NICOLLET ISLAND (page 26)

LARGEST LITE-BRITE (page 64)

LONGFELLOW GARDENS (page 48)

HOT SAM'S ANTIQUES AND FOTO PARK (page 2)

WASHBURN PARK WATER TOWER (page 82)

In this new place, this new man, built family in bohemian flats and buildings with his hands

SHADOWS OF SPIRIT (page 14)

LIMB MAKERS

Which legendary Twin Cities company uses a robot named Robert to sculpt artificial limbs?

Minneapolis is well known for its milling, logging, and railroad legacies. But because of all the work-related accidents in those industries, the city also became a notable hub for artificial limb entrepreneurs. One such pioneer was Albert Winkley.

An amputee himself, Winkley set a new standard for comfort when he invented a double-slip socket prosthesis. His company, founded in 1888 with Lowell Jepson, is now the largest family-owned orthopedic and prosthetics company in the nation. With headquarters in the suburb of Golden Valley, Winkley Orthotics & Prosthetics is owned by Jepson's great-great-grandchildren Alex and Amalia, the fifth generation of the family to own the business.

In the beginning, artificial limbs were made of wood by craftsmen such as cabinetmakers, clockmakers, and locksmiths. As demand for limbs grew during and after World Wars I and II, the industry changed dramatically. Fortunately, doctors who took over limb amputation and reconstruction realized the need for padding between the patient's bone and the artificial limb. Eventually the industry switched to plastics, resulting in more comfortable and realistic-looking products.

The technology continues to grow more sophisticated. In the late 1990s and early 2000s, microprocessor knees were introduced. They feature computerized sensors in the joint to help detect and stabilize movement. And now with

In addition to the needs of war veterans, the demand for artificial limbs in Minneapolis grew because of all the limbs lost during milling, logging, farming, and railroad accidents.

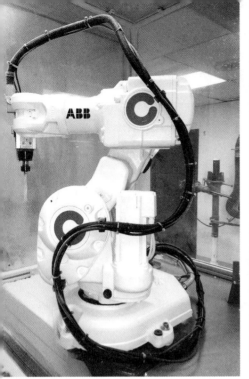

Winkley Orthotics & Prosthetics, the oldest privately owned orthotics and prosthetics company in the country, was founded in 1888. Now headquartered in Golden Valley, it remains a leader in technology, using microprocessors and a sculpting robot.

smartphones, users can control the settings and switch between modes, such as standing, driving, or walking up and down stairs. Winkley is also home to a five-foot-tall, seven-axis robot arm carver (named Robert). Swiveling from side to side, Robert sculpts the fine details of bones and arches with precision. It's one of only a few robotic carvers used in the industry nationwide.

WINKLEY ORTHOTICS & PROSTHETICS

WHAT One of the original artificial limb pioneers still in operation today

WHERE Winkley headquarters, 740 Douglas Dr. N., Golden Valley

COST Free to stop in and see the historical photos in the lobby. Tours by appointment.

PRO TIP Winkley now has eight other locations in Minnesota and Wisconsin.

OLD DIVES AND PIG'S EYE

Where can you win a slab of meat for a dollar while paying homage to Saint Paul's dubious origin?

The Spot Bar in West Seventh—Saint Paul's first neighborhood—is the classic dimly lit hole-in-the-wall. It features pull tabs, pinball, darts, hotdish cook-offs, cribbage tournaments, Hamm's beer, an occasional vintage clothing sale, and a Friday night meat raffle touted as "the Wildest on the Wild West End." For those of you not from these parts, a meat raffle is a quintessential Minnesotan tradition and viewed by some as the greatest event ever to take place in a bar.

Located in a building dating back to 1885, The Spot tells the story of Saint Paul almost better than any museum could. For starters, the interior—now featuring decades-old articles on the wall and a little library in the back where there used to be an organ—has hardly changed since the streets outside were filled with horses and buggies. But the real kicker is the barn-like exterior with the old Pig's Eye Pilsner Beer sign featuring the guy with a patch.

Pig's Eye is what the capital city used to be named before a priest came along and changed it to Saint Paul. The name Pig's Eye originated with Pierre Parrant (the guy with the patch), a dodgy bootlegger considered the first European settler to inhabit the city's borders. His bad

---

THE SPOT BAR, PIG'S EYE, AND FOUNTAIN CAVE

WHAT A legendary old dive bar and the legacy of the one-eyed fella on the sign

WHERE 859 Randolph Ave., Saint Paul

COST $1 per meat raffle ticket

PRO TIP Built in 1885, The Spot is one of the bars that claims it's the oldest bar in Minnesota. Neumann's in North Saint Paul also makes a strong case for that title.

The Pig's Eye Pilsner Beer sign attached to The Spot Bar features Pierre Parrant, a one-eyed fella "of dubious reputation." Although he was evicted from Saint Paul in 1845, he's considered the city's first European settler and business entrepreneur.

eye apparently had a white ring around the pupil, giving it a kind of piggish expression.

In 1838, Pierre "Pig's Eye" Parrant built a saloon, Saint Paul's first business, at the entrance of Fountain Cave about a half mile from where The Spot now stands. According to the National Park Service website, "a 150-foot-long winding hall in the cave led to a beautiful circular room about fifty feet in diameter." Later, the cave was used as a storehouse and then as a tourist attraction. Eventually, the entrance was buried by construction. A historical marker is located on the bike path on the bluff above the cave location, just off Shepard Road.

With its dubious origin revolving around a one-eyed bootlegger combined with the influx of thirsty Bavarians starting in the 1850s, it's no wonder Saint Paul has grown up with a thriving dive bar culture.

CLUB MED FOR SWANS

Why do hordes of trumpeter swans, once on the brink of extinction, now flock to the same spot near a nuclear plant each winter?

For some, winter is the perfect time to sit by the fire and read books. For others, it's the perfect time to travel forty miles northwest of Minneapolis to view one of the largest flocks of trumpeter swans in the Midwest. Each winter, as many as three thousand congregate at a little park on a dead-end street in Monticello. Why? Because of an intricate sequence of events over many years that boils down to this: the stars aligned.

First there's the patch of Mississippi River that doesn't freeze due to the nearby nuclear-power generating plant. Next, as part of a statewide restoration effort launched by Three Rivers Park District in the 1960s, the DNR imported 150 trumpeter swan eggs from Alaska, over a three-year period, in the 1980s. A mated pair from the first delivery was given to the Minnesota Zoo. After a couple of years, the pair was released into the wild.

As the released pair was flying up the river, the spunky alpha female (known as Seven) spotted local resident Sheila Lawrence feeding corn to geese and ducks from the shores of her backyard in those nuclear-warmed

SWAN PARK

WHAT A narrow stretch of the Mississippi River that's become a wildly popular winter vacation spot for trumpeter swans

WHERE 121 Mississippi Dr., Monticello

COST Free, although donations to keep feeding the swans at the Monticello site are collected through the Swan City Heritage Foundation.

PRO TIP During mild winters, the swan count is lower. Before traveling to Monticello, check the city swan update at monticellocci.com/pages/swans. They can also be seen on Monticello's live swan cam at fibernetmonticello.com/swan-cam.

Featured in the photo by Lommel Photography is the late Sheila Lawrence, affectionately dubbed "The Swan Lady." Photo courtesy of Sheila's husband, Jim Lawrence.

waters. Accustomed to being fed by humans at the zoo, Seven swooped in and helped herself. Because Seven was considered a boss in the swan world, she enticed several other swans to join the feast that winter too.

As the weather warmed, all the mated swans departed to their nesting sites in thawed marshes, ponds, and lakes. The next winter (and every winter since), they returned to Sheila's corn buffet with new broods. To keep up, Sheila and her husband, Jim, installed a conveyor feeding system. Affectionately dubbed "The Swan Lady," Sheila died in 2011. Her final request to Jim ("The Swan Guy") was "Will you feed my swans?" He and/or his son have been doing so ever since at 10:30 a.m. every day from early December until spring.

While honking and flapping their magnificent, pure-white wings, the trumpeter swans that gather each winter in Monticello sound like a room full of sixth graders warming up for their first band concert.

THE SMILING BUILDING

Why does Marquette Plaza look like it's smiling?

You almost can't help but smile back at it. Designed in 1972, the fifteen-story Marquette Plaza in downtown Minneapolis was the first building in the world to use a cable support system similar to the kind used in suspension bridges. What looks like a giant glass smile reflecting across its exterior is a band of steel cables hanging in a U shape, technically called a catenary curve. Each end is secured to the outside concrete towers.

Why the U-shaped cables? The building was originally designed as headquarters for the Federal Reserve Bank. The above-ground levels needed to be open and sunny while the money vault below needed to be extremely secure. Designer Gunnar Birkerts used catenary cables to support the upper part. By doing so, the need for columns that would've posed problems for the underground vault was eliminated.

Although the building's design was highly praised, it was plagued with defects, including asbestos. The Federal Reserve Bank moved to a new complex nearby in 1997. The building sat

MARQUETTE PLAZA AND CANCER SURVIVORS PARK

WHAT The story behind an iconic downtown building and its front lawn sculpture

WHERE 250 Marquette Ave. S., Minneapolis

COST Free

PRO TIP Go to blochcancer.org to learn about the Richard & Annette Bloch Family Foundation, represented by the Cancer Survivors Park in front of Marquette Plaza.

The front lawn of Marquette Plaza, featuring the 1.5-acre Cancer Survivors Park, reflects the same U shape featured on the front of the building.

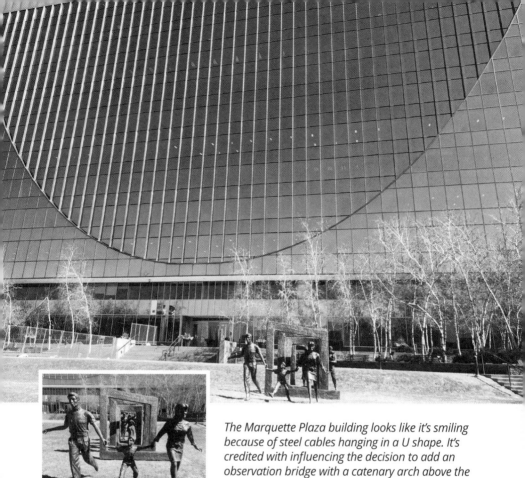

The Marquette Plaza building looks like it's smiling because of steel cables hanging in a U shape. It's credited with influencing the decision to add an observation bridge with a catenary arch above the dramatic opening in Saudi Arabia's Kingdom Centre.

empty until a developer bought it in 2000 and overhauled it. The Minneapolis Public Library occupied it for a few years. Then private tenants moved in.

The grassy area in front of the building was designed to reflect the same curved shape. That area includes the Cancer Survivors Park, sponsored by the Richard & Annette Bloch Family Foundation. The sculpture, titled *Cancer . . . There's Hope*, is the last work of the world-renowned sculptor Victor Salmones. The five figures in the back walking toward the maze-like structure represent cancer patients and their supporters preparing to enter treatment. The front three figures represent the joy of successful treatment. Also in the park is a Positive Mental Attitude Walk and a Road to Recovery with plaques of advice and encouragement.

REMEMBERING RONDO

Where can you pay tribute to a legendary neighborhood demolished to make way for Interstate 94?

The Rondo neighborhood in Saint Paul was once the heart of the city's African American community. While redlining practices kept them from buying homes in certain neighborhoods, Rondo was a welcoming place where they could take pride in homeownership, start businesses, publish newspapers, and fully participate in cultural, social, and civil rights activities. But in 1956, construction of Interstate 94 to connect the downtown areas of Minneapolis and Saint Paul tore through the neighborhood.

Hundreds of homes and businesses were obliterated, disrupting the lives of thousands. Those impacted, however, have continued to work together to keep the neighborhood's spirit alive. In 1982, Marvin Anderson and Floyd Smaller launched Rondo Avenue Incorporated, an organization dedicated to sharing the contributions of African Americans and the neighborhood's rich history. Their initiatives include Rondo Days—a large, annual weekend festival held in mid-July. They also advocated for the new Rondo Commemorative Plaza, on Old Rondo Avenue, that had its grand opening in 2018.

The humble plaza features an exhibit wall that tells the Rondo story. In the center is a grassy mound symbolizing rising

The Rondo neighborhood was home to many legends, including Roy Wilkins, a prominent activist in the civil rights movement, and Toni Stone, the first of three women to play professional baseball as a part of the Negro League.

While the construction of I-94 erased the Rondo neighborhood, its vibrant spirit lives on. In 2018, a commemorative plaza was completed to educate others about the Rondo story and to celebrate its legacy.

RONDO COMMEMORATIVE PLAZA

WHAT Tribute to a legendary neighborhood torn apart by I-94

WHERE 820 Concordia Ave./Old Rondo Ave., Saint Paul

COST Free

PRO TIP A student-produced documentary called *Rondo: Beyond the Pavement* chronicles the history of the Rondo neighborhood through interviews with elders who lived the story. Check it out at rondobeyondthepavement.org.

dreams from devastation. At one end is an installation of eighteen chimes, each dedicated to one of the eighteen north–south streets that ran through Rondo. On the plaza's northeast corner is a tower with a lighted beacon visible to drivers passing by on I-94. On July 17, 2015, Chris Coleman, Saint Paul's mayor at the time, issued an apology on behalf of the city "for our sins of the past." He also declared July 17 as "Rondo Remembrance and Reconciliation Day" in Saint Paul.

FRANK'S FISH FASCINATION

Which three local gems were designed by the same Frank and inspired by fish splashing around in his grandmother's bathtub?

If the Weisman Art Museum on the University of Minnesota campus looks to you like a twisted blend of water splashes and fish scales against the glare of the sun, you're not imagining it. Ever since he was a young boy, world-famous architect Frank Gehry, known for his unusual fabrications, has been a bit fish obsessed.

Born to Russian and Polish Jewish parents in Canada, Gehry would often build imaginary buildings and cities from items found in his grandfather's hardware store. His fascination with the movement of the fish body began when he and his grandmother would travel to the Jewish market each Thursday. She'd buy a big carp and put it in her bathtub until it was time to turn it into gefilte, a traditional Jewish appetizer. Gehry would watch it twist and turn in the water for hours, completely mesmerized.

In addition to the Weisman Art Museum, there are two other local structures created by Gehry. One is a fish lamp. The other is the long-adored, floor-to-ceiling, sea-green fish sculpture known as *Standing Glass Fish*. They both currently reside at the Weisman.

Many works of architect Frank Gehry, who changed his name from Frank Owen Goldberg to avoid anti-Semitism, are influenced by time spent in his grandfather's hardware store and watching fish flop around in his grandmother's bathtub.

With the Mississippi River as its backdrop, the shimmering and "scaly" Weisman Art Museum, completed in 1993, provides a fresh, engaging arts experience for the University of Minnesota and the community.

ARCHITECT FRANK GEHRY'S "FISHY" FABRICATIONS

WHAT The inspiration behind the architect's shimmering and fish-like structures in Minneapolis

WHERE Weisman Art Museum, 333 E. River Pkwy., Minneapolis

COST Free

PRO TIP Parking, for a fee, is available under the museum.

Standing Glass Fish used to be located inside the Cowles Conservatory at the Minneapolis Sculpture Garden on the grounds of the Walker Art Center. But as the Sculpture Garden underwent a massive renovation in recent years, it was decided that the conservatory was too expensive to heat in the winter, so it was turned into an open pavilion. *Standing Glass Fish* needed a new home. Fittingly, it was carefully taken apart, fish scale by fish scale, and reassembled at the Weisman Art Museum on a long-term loan.

BRIDGE TO NOWHERE

Why does that bridge stop halfway across the Mississippi? And who was once chased across it by the FBI?

Although Inver Grove Heights, a southeast suburb of Minneapolis, is situated along the Mississippi River, there aren't many public places to get up close to the river in that area. There are a couple of spots to check out the spectacular views from above, though. One of them is the bridge-like structure at Swing Bridge Park.

Unlike normal bridges that help you get to the other side of something, this one abruptly stops halfway across the river. As with most oddities, it's got quite a story to it. The tale of gangster John Dillinger, who once used it as an escape route during a gun battle with the FBI (when it was a full-length bridge, of course), is only part of it.

Built in 1894 and known as the Rock Island Swing Bridge, it was originally designed as a double-deck structure. It carried trains on the top deck and vehicles on the lower deck to and from Saint Paul Park. When it was a full-length bridge at 1,661 feet, it was among the longest of its kind in the world. In 1982, it was closed to trains, and in 1999, it was closed to all traffic after being judged unsafe. It was then slated for demolition in 2008.

After a two-hundred-foot span of the bridge fell into the river and other spans of it were intentionally removed, demolition was halted. Instead, a decision was made to turn

---

After part of it fell into the river, the Rock Island Swing Bridge was named one of the state's "Ten Most Endangered Historic Places." Now it's a recreational pier dangling halfway over the river.

Walking to the end of the bridge, now a pier, is a great way to appreciate the river while reveling in history. There's a bench at the end where you can sit and watch the sunset. Right at the entrance to the pier is a one-flight staircase to a scenic outlook for even more incredible views.

ROCK ISLAND SWING BRIDGE

WHAT A former double-decker bridge that's now a pier extending halfway out into the Mississippi River

WHERE Swing Bridge Park, 4465 Sixty-Sixth St. E., Inver Grove Heights

COST Free

PRO TIP A trailhead facility is also located at this park that connects to the Mississippi River Regional Trail between Saint Paul and Hastings. The facility includes an air pump for bikes, restrooms, water, and benches.

the remaining spans into a 670-foot recreational pier. As luck would have it, eighteen months into the renovation process, the bridge caught fire from nearby welding sparks in 2010. But thanks to liability insurance, the completed pier (with an end cap to keep people from falling off the edge) is now a popular spot for wedding and prom photos, walkers, cyclists, and history buffs.

SAINTLY FUN

Where were thousands of fans given whoopee cushions and encouraged to sit down on them at the same time?

Minor league baseball is known for its unusual promotions and antics. But the Saint Paul Saints, with a live costumed pig that delivers balls as their mascot, take it to another level. You'd expect nothing less, though, with co-owners like Mike Veeck, "the comic maestro of the minor leagues," and Bill Murray, acclaimed actor and comedian. Murray is also listed as the team's "psychologist." Their mantra? "Fun is Good!"

From instigating world record pillow fights to creating the world's largest Twister game by spraying fifty thousand colored circles onto its field, the team keeps you guessing upon entering CHS Field—the Saints' $65 million home in Saint Paul's Lowertown Art District.

SAINT PAUL SAINTS

WHAT The wackiest team in all of minor league baseball

WHERE CHS Field, 360 Broadway St. N., Saint Paul

COST Most seats $14–$16; behind-the-scenes tour at CHS Field $15-$19

PRO TIP During Friday, Saturday, and Sunday home games, the Saints offer free all-age art activities and demonstrations by local artists. Look for the Traveling Art Cart on the concourse or at the Saints Art Tent by the Kids Corner.

One time, they handed out rain gear and packs of mashed potatoes for an epic ballpark-wide food fight to celebrate the fortieth anniversary of *Animal House*. Another time they gave out whoopee cushions, then encouraged the nearly seven thousand fans in attendance to stand up and sit down on the cushions all at the same time. Take a second to imagine those lovely acoustics. They also have a history of sending fans home with clever gifts, such as bobblehead dolls, rubber boats, and boxer shorts that often poke fun at misbehaving politicians and celebrities.

You never know what's going to happen next inside CHS Field, home of the Saint Paul Saints in Lowertown. Whether it's on the field hosting some crazy promotion or out in the stands talking to the fans, this team knows how to have fun. As co-owner Mike Veeck says, "Fun is Good!"

While the guys on the field play to win, the club surely has earned its reputation as one of the most fun, high-energy experiences in Saint Paul. It also infuses the surrounding neighborhood's artistic spirit. Walk around the concourse and check out the kiosks reserved for local artists and the spectacular city view behind left field.

"Except for your own child's team ballgame, it's the most fun baseball experience that is possible in the United States of America and in the world." —Bill Murray, as featured on the Saints' official trailer

THE CITY'S ATTIC

What treasures are hidden inside the Minneapolis City Hall clock tower?

Through the ages, clock towers have had a certain mystique about them, earning cameos in legendary sci-fi and fantasy films. The nineteenth-century clock tower atop Minneapolis's City Hall and Hennepin County Courthouse has its fair share of fascination too.

Not only because its face is six inches larger than London's Big Ben. Not only because the bells once filled the downtown skies with Prince songs and can play "The Star-Spangled Banner" in the original key (with the help of a keyboard in the first-floor rotunda). But also because tucked away in the bottom floors of the 345-foot clock tower are hundreds of thousands of historical records that hardly anyone ever sees.

The space occupies 4,714 square feet in six tiers. Nearly every inch is packed with materials detailing the city's history and government activities back to the 1850s. Giant books with criminal and fire logs handwritten on crinkly paper. Maps. School yearbooks. Theater programs. WWII propaganda posters. Boxes of historic photographs. Editorial cartoons. Petitions to oust a long-ago mayor and police chief. Even a rodent control campaign to drive rats out of the city. Although it's an uncatalogued jumble, it's a historian's dream house overseen by a small city staff.

Because the room lacks temperature and humidity controls, a portion of the photographs and maps has been donated to

Fun fact: In the early 1900s, the Minneapolis City Hall and Courthouse also rented space to a blacksmith shop, a horse stable, a wool brokerage, and a chicken hatchery.

Although hardly anyone ever sees it, the inside of the Minneapolis City Hall's big, drafty clock tower might be the coolest place in town. It's an uncatalogued, haphazard treasure trove of historical documents, books, and photos, some dating back to the 1850s.

the Hennepin County Library over the years to ensure their long-term preservation. To make those materials more accessible to the public, the library has initiated a massive effort to digitize tens of thousands of images with the help of volunteers. Those efforts can now be accessed online through HCL's digital collections.

MINNEAPOLIS CITY ARCHIVES IN CLOCK TOWER

WHAT A treasure trove of historical records stored in the City Hall's clock tower

WHERE City Hall, 350 S. Fifth St., Minneapolis

COST Free to tour City Hall (clock tower not open to the public)

PRO TIP While on a self-guided tour of City Hall, rub the big toe of the partially nude *Father of Waters* statue in the City Hall rotunda for good luck. Also, near the elevators on the ground floor, look for the face carved into the marble that's sticking out its tongue.

FROM THE LAND OF TRAPEZE

Where can you check "Flying Trapeze" off your bucket list inside a legendary old brewery warehouse?

Mention the word Hamm's to nostalgic beer-loving Minnesotans, and immediately they launch into that catchy song from those old-time commercials—the one that featured a potbellied, dancing bear. First comes the tom-tom beat and then:

> *From the land of sky-blue waters (waaaaa-ters),*
> *From the land of pines, lofty balsams*
> *Comes the beer refreshing,*
> *Hamm's the beer refreshing . . .*
> *Hmmm . . . Hamm's!*

Once the nation's fifth-largest beer company, Theodore Hamm's Brewing Company (which later became Stroh's) closed its doors after operating for 130 years on Dayton's Bluff overlooking Saint Paul. Most of its fifty-four buildings are still standing. While many are crumbling and vacant, some are bustling with new businesses. Tucked inside a warehouse on the north side of the property is a trapeze school.

In 2013, Katie Kimball decided the cavernous ceilings and sunshine flooding through the multipaned windows created the perfect place to teach people how to fly. Kimball, a dancer and expert aerial artist, gained her education in the performance, safety, and equipment elements of trapeze arts in Oakland,

---

After sitting vacant for decades, the legendary old Hamm's Brewery is becoming a hot hub for creative tenants, from painters and photographers to chocolatiers and trapeze artists.

People of all abilities are coaxed off the ledge inside one of the abandoned buildings on the north side of the old Hamm's Brewery campus.

California. And now, back in her home state, she's the one coaxing people off the ledge.

Some participants are regulars. For others, it's a one-time deal. Novices begin by hanging from their knees on the low bar. Then, it's up the narrow, two-story ladder. Kimball's cat Ringling, who lives there, will often be purring and watching from below. Once on the platform, safety harnesses are attached. Last-minute instructions are given. Katie or one of the other instructors says "Ready?" Then "Hep!" That's the cue. After leaping off the edge, the goal is for participants to lift their knees up, hook them around the fly bar, and connect hands with the professional catcher mid-air. There is, of course, a great big safety net below.

HAMM'S BREWERY AND THE TWIN CITIES TRAPEZE CENTER

WHAT Trapeze classes for all levels in a former Hamm's Brewery warehouse

WHERE 719 E. Minnehaha Ave., Saint Paul

COST $50 for each ninety-minute session

PRO TIP A couple of other places in the Twin Cities teach trapeze, including the Circus Juventus for youth, but the Twin Cities Trapeze Center is the only school that offers a one-time beginner's class for kids and adults.

G'S LAST CASTLE

ch mansion was used as a mortuary, a restaurant, school, and a scene in a cult classic film?

With its grand parlors, secret passageways, third-floor ballroom, and spooky cellar, the H. Alden Smith estate—connected to the Minneapolis Community & Technical College (MCTC)—is the only survivor among the nineteenth-century mansions that once circled Loring Park. Bigwigs like the Pillsburys and Washburns used to party there. It was built in 1887 for Smith, co-owner of the Smith & Wyman Sash and Door Company that once boomed in Minneapolis. Since Smith and his wife died more than a century ago, it has housed some surprising endeavors and been cloaked in ghostly lore.

For over fifty years, the home functioned as Davies Mortuary. The estate's kitchen was transformed into an embalming room. After that, for a short time, it was used for a bar and restaurant called The Little Prince. In 1991, the interior of the mansion appeared as a therapist's office in the comedy-drama film *Drop Dead Fred*, starring Carrie Fisher and Phoebe Cates. From 1993 to 2018, the mansion was owned by MCTC, which renamed it the Wells Family College Center. The college used the space for meetings and outreach programs, including a computer-training program for senior citizens.

Throughout all these transitions, people have reported strange observations. The elevator going up and down on its own.

The H. Alden Smith Mansion, which has housed some surprising endeavors and been cloaked in ghostly lore, is the last survivor of the nineteenth-century mansions that once circled Loring Park.

Today, the historic H. Alden Smith Mansion is nearly surrounded by the Minneapolis Community & Technical College, which owned the property from 1993 to 2018.

H. ALDEN SMITH MANSION

WHAT Quirky scoop on the last remaining mansion on the perimeter of Loring Park

WHERE 1403 Harmon Pl., Minneapolis

COST Free

PRO TIP The mansion is a short walk to the intriguing Berger Fountain (a.k.a. "The Dandelion Fountain"). The fountain was donated to Loring Park by Parks Commissioner Ben Berger. He paid for it with the money he earned selling popcorn during 1973 screenings of *The Exorcist* at a local movie theater he owned.

Doors slamming. Radios randomly turning on. Some bats. A phantom woman looking out the window. Bulletin board memos flying upward with no breeze in site. And the smell of cut flowers wafting through vacant rooms and outside the property in January.

The college was "not well-positioned" to manage such a historic building. After estimating it would require several million dollars of renovations to adequately meet its needs, MCTC sold it for $1 to a developer. It's now being restored and linked to a new residential apartment complex on the adjacent land.

127

STORIES ON WHEELS

What's that bright red, bubble-top, buggy thing parked over there?

While walking through the museums, festivals, and neighborhoods of Saint Paul, you might encounter a cherry-red vehicle that looks like the aero car some of us remember from *The Jetsons* cartoon show. Except it has wheels. Marked with a Storymobile logo, it's actually a solar-powered audio/film studio that travels around town to record and archive people's life stories. Equipped with iPads, cameras, microphones, amps, keyboards, and good old paper and pencils, its purpose is to collect personal narratives across cultures and generations in Saint Paul.

Storymobile is the brainchild of Saint Paul Almanac, a nonprofit literary arts organization. Artist Roger Cummings and Saint Paul Public School students designed and manufactured Storymobile 1.0. Later, Cummings and other artists designed a newer version, Storymobile 2.0.

Writers, artists, and filmmakers staff Storymobile and help participants record their stories. The storytellers can receive an electronic copy of their stories and have the option to submit them to a special collection at local libraries and for possible inclusion in Saint Paul Almanac's annual publication. Storymobile is also available to rent for special events, such as block parties and family reunions. So far, two thousand stories have been gathered across the metro area.

The solar-powered, roving art space travels behind an electric, egg-shaped bicycle to collect and record community stories.

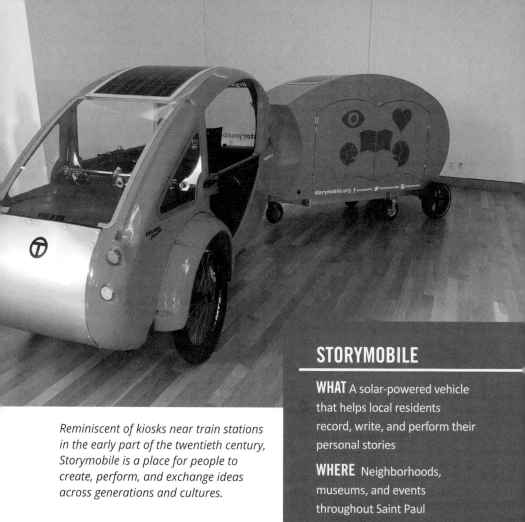

Reminiscent of kiosks near train stations in the early part of the twentieth century, Storymobile is a place for people to create, perform, and exchange ideas across generations and cultures.

STORYMOBILE

WHAT A solar-powered vehicle that helps local residents record, write, and perform their personal stories

WHERE Neighborhoods, museums, and events throughout Saint Paul

COST Free on the street. For special events, they offer a sliding scale.

PRO TIP Click on the news tab at saintpaulalmanac.org for newsletters announcing upcoming appearances.

In November 2017, after collecting stories at Immanuel Lutheran Church's sixty-eighth annual lutefisk dinner, Storymobile went missing. It had been parked on the street in the Summit-University neighborhood. An anonymous donor pledged a $500 reward for information leading to its safe return. On Thanksgiving morning, a Good Samaritan found it across town in an alley. "Other than a couple clipped wires, a broken chain, and a stolen spare wheel, the trailer was intact," according to the *Star Tribune*. And fortunately, the stories had all been saved to the cloud.

OLD-TIME CINEMA

Which movie theater has a century-old organ that rises out of the floor before weekend movies?

Those who appreciate old-time charm and real butter on their popcorn will love the Heights Theater, located in the Northeast suburb of Columbia Heights. The moment you stand in front of the Italian Renaissance brick building and look up at its sparkling tower atop a marquee, you know you're in for a magical experience.

A grand piano and an old projector are on display in the elegant lobby. Antique chandeliers with Egyptian crystals hang from the ceilings in the auditorium. Hand-painted bulbs in four colors add to the ambience. Scarlet curtains drape across the stage. And a spectacular organ that rises out of the orchestra pit provides unique music before weekend movies.

Opened in 1926 by Arthur Gluek of the Gluek Brewery family, Heights Theater is the oldest continuously operating movie theater in Minnesota. Because films were silent back then, a small pipe organ provided the soundtrack. But after more sophisticated sound technology came along, the organ was removed. When Dave Holmgren and Tom Letness bought the theater in 1998, they restored the theater to its original glory. In doing so, they discovered a hidden orchestra pit in front of the stage. So they brought in an organ again with the help of the Land O'Lakes Chapter of the American Theatre Organ Society.

The Heights Theater has survived at least three fires, one bombing, and "The Big Blow of 1949" when a tornado twisted the tower sign.

The former 1929 Wurlitzer Pipe Organ of Radio Station WCCO now rises out of the floor at the historic Heights Theater in Columbia Heights, offering movie guests unique music.

THE HEIGHTS THEATER

WHAT The first movie theater in the Twin Cities area to offer live organ music since the 1950s

WHERE 3951 Central Ave. NE, Columbia Heights

COST $10-$12 per ticket

PRO TIP The owner of the Heights also owns the Dairy Queen next door. That means moviegoers get DQ coupons and are allowed to carry a Blizzard into the theater.

The current organ dates back to 1929 when it was used as the WCCO studio organ. Now before the evening show on Fridays and Saturdays, the organ rises out of the orchestra pit and a rotating group of organists play a short program. Tom Letness, who became sole owner of the Heights Theater in 2003, specializes in upscale first-run films and classic film series.

CARNIES' RESTING PLACE

Where is there a burial plot area reserved for carnival and circus workers?

Although it holds more than two hundred thousand human remains, there's nothing creepy about Lakewood Cemetery. Located on the southern end of Uptown Minneapolis, it's more like a serene sculpture garden.

With 250 acres of rolling hills, reflecting pools, symbolic monuments, and a Memorial Chapel with glorious acoustics and mosaic artwork, it's long been known as one of America's most spectacular cemeteries. Everybody knows it's the go-to place for paying respects to Minnesota's most famous leaders and influencers. But did you know Section 28 has a plot area reserved for behind-the-scenes circus and carnival workers?

It's nothing fancy. Called Showmen's Rest, it features a few trees, shrubs, and a granite slab engraved with a three-stanza poem to commemorate them. But it's a thoughtful remembrance of those often born and raised in the business, moving from town to town with trucks and trailers, cleaning up after elephants, and operating merry-go-rounds. "Everybody buried here did something for this business to keep it going and make it what it is," said Mike Featherstone, chairman of the Midwest Showmen's Association during an on-site Minnesota Public Radio segment.

"Did you enjoy a thrill, a laugh? Then let this be our epitaph . . ." That's just one of the great lines from the three-stanza poem on a granite slab commemorating carnival and circus workers buried at Lakewood Cemetery.

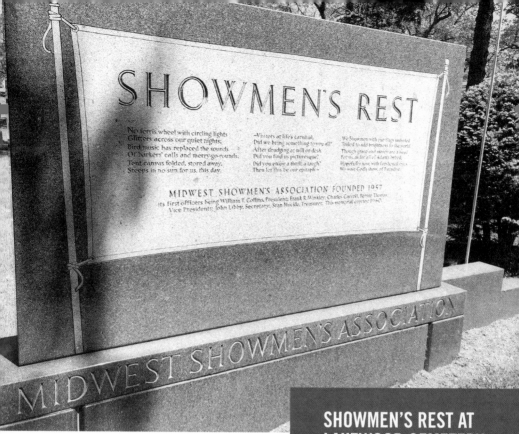

Showmen's Rest was established in 1960 as a final resting place for those who made their career doing behind-the-scenes grunt work at carnivals and circuses.

Also at the cemetery are the remains of Herbert Buckingham Khaury, the ukulele-playing, falsetto-voiced entertainer known as Tiny Tim. He died of a heart attack in 1996 while on stage at the Woman's Club of Minneapolis singing his hit "Tiptoe through the Tulips." Upon entering the cemetery, turn right. You'll find his tomb in the lower level of the second mausoleum. He's entombed with his ukulele, six tulips, and a stuffed rabbit.

SHOWMEN'S REST AT LAKEWOOD CEMETERY (AND TINY TIM)

WHAT Plot at Lakewood Cemetery dedicated to carnival and circus workers

WHERE Section 28 of Lakewood Cemetery, 3600 Hennepin Ave., Minneapolis

COST Free

PRO TIP Download the Lakewood Cemetery app for maps, tours, and a search feature to find any grave you want. A self-guided tour is available on its website.

HARRIET PLAYGROUND PORTRAIT

What's the story behind the rusted, pixelated portrait on the Harriet Island playground?

Harriet Island, no longer an island since the back channel was filled in, was once home to public baths and a zoo. Now it's a lovely place to experience the Mississippi riverfront. Hop on a riverboat cruise. Sleep overnight in a vintage towboat bed-and-breakfast. Enjoy a concert amidst otters and bald eagles. Read stone tributes honoring war veterans. And come face-to-face with a large, weathered, pixelated portrait of a frontier woman mounted on the playground.

If you're not familiar with who she is, you may think the portrait looks . . . well, a little out of place. (The same image hangs on a wall at the Saint Paul Grill.) For your information, she is Harriet Bishop, the city's first schoolteacher, for whom the island was named. A school, excursion steamer, and trolley car were also named for her.

In 1847, Bishop moved from the East Coast to Saint Paul—a raw river town at the time—to open the city's first public school in a former blacksmith's shop at what's now the corner of St. Peter Street and Kellogg Boulevard. The structure consisted of mud walls and a few snakes and rats. For a touch of comfort, Bishop upholstered the sparse furniture with her own needlepoint. But Bishop, strong willed and adventurous, was

Although she was not a Minnesota native, Bishop described it as her home: "I have known Minnesota from its infancy and have loved it as a parent does a child." (Source: South History Archive by Lois Glewwe at dakotahistory.org.)

The memory of Harriet Bishop—an American educator, writer, suffragist, temperance activist, and Minnesota's first schoolteacher—is honored today in several places. One of them is on the playground at Harriet Island.

no simple schoolmarm. She was a founding member of the town's first Baptist Church, the Home for the Friendless, the Woman's Christian Temperance Union, and the Minnesota Woman Suffrage Association.

Speaking of women's suffrage, did you know the first woman in the United States to vote after passage of the Nineteenth Amendment, which technically granted women the right to vote, was from South Saint Paul? It was Marguerite Newburgh, who voted in South Saint Paul's waterworks bond election the morning after the amendment was certified as law on August 26, 1920.

WEATHERBALL TRIBUTES

Where did Twin Citians often look for weather updates long before iPhones came along?

Understandably, checking for weather updates is a widespread pastime in the Twin Cities. So much so that in 1949, Northwestern National Bank in downtown Minneapolis (where the Wells Fargo Tower now stands) installed a 157-foot-high, seventy-eight-ton weatherball on its roof. Wrapped in one and a quarter miles of neon tubing and accentuated with the bank's initials, the beacon was visible from fifteen miles away at night.

With a direct line to the National Weather Service, lights inside the glass sphere changed to red, green, white, or blinking, according to the forecast. A sing-along advertising jingle helped people remember the color-coded system. To hear it, you can push a button on the vibrant weatherball replica at the Wells Fargo Center skyway-level history museum.

The weatherball was so popular that Northwest distributed Mr. Weatherball coin banks to customers. Unfortunately, on Thanksgiving Day in 1982, a fire started by arsonists destroyed an entire block of downtown Minneapolis, including the Northwestern National Bank Building. The weatherball was brought safely to the ground, though, with a helicopter and crane. The plan was

A mini-replica of the Weatherball on display at the Wells Fargo history museum and the WCCO Weather Watcher help keep the spirit of the beloved old beacon alive.

to relocate it to the State Fair. Instead, it collected dust in storage and finally met its end at the scrapyard.

As a salute to the weatherball, WCCO-TV introduced the Weather Watcher in 2013. The one-hundred-foot beacon stands on the station's lovely landscaped rooftop studio, along with a full-service outdoor kitchen, fire pit, seating area, and garden space. Instead of a ball, the station's logo letters provide the color for the forecast. Red means warmer weather ahead. Blue means colder. Green means snow or rain. White signals no change. For urgent weather warnings, meteorologists can also make the colors flash with a click of a button.

The Northwestern National Bank Weatherball, once the largest bank sign between Chicago and the West Coast, was the first in a series of weather-reporting beacons that dotted the skylines of cities across the United States.

ONCE THERE WERE FROGS

Which Saint Paul neighborhood has the least amount of green space but one of the largest urban organic farms in the country?

Even with a nickname like Frogtown, it's hard to imagine that the bustling, inner-city Thomas-Dale neighborhood in Saint Paul was once a swampy wetland with little amphibians all over the place croaking the night away. These days, it's rich in cultural diversity but sorely lacking in green space. In fact, it's got less green space per child than anywhere in the city.

However, thanks to community-wide grassroots efforts, including everything from frog-focused science education and butterfly gardens to park clean-ups and tree plantings, that's changing. And at the heart of it all is a one-of-a-kind, thirteen-acre park with five acres devoted to an organic farm, collectively known as Frogtown Park and Farm.

The farm area, open to the public since 2013, is leased from the city of Saint Paul by the nonprofit group Frogtown Farm. In 2009, the Wilder Foundation, a social service provider in Saint Paul, moved its headquarters out of the area. This opened up a rare patch of land. Local advocates wasted no time in

---

"When neighbors plant, weed, harvest, cook, or participate in programs at Frogtown Farm, they share stories, knowledge, and culture. Through farming, art, and food, those stories nourish us and help to develop relationships across race, class, gender, and generation." (Source: Frogtown Farm newsletter.)

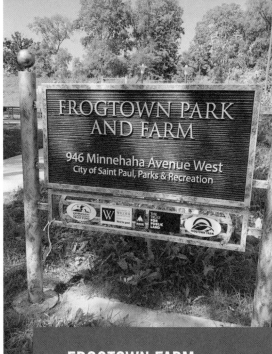

Frogtown is a densely populated neighborhood with a large Hmong and Lao community, located along University Avenue between Lexington Avenue and I-35. At the heart of it is Frogtown Farm, which supplies locally grown food to neighborhood restaurants, markets, community groups, and families.

FROGTOWN FARM

WHAT One of the largest urban organic farms in the country

WHERE 946 W. Minnehaha Ave., Saint Paul

COST Free to stroll through the farm

PRO TIP Look for the courtyard on one end of the farm dedicated to the Sisters of the Good Shepherd. From 1883 to 1969, the Sisters operated a refuge on this sacred ground for young women and girls who were orphaned, homeless, or at risk.

contacting the Trust for Public Land to purchase the land for an urban park and farm.

It features fields, a hoop house, and an outdoor kitchen. As one of the largest organic urban farms in the nation, it's a wonderful place for residents to come together to plant, weed, and harvest; gain more affordable access to fresh produce; learn about the importance of food and cooking; and share stories over baked bread and wood-fired pizza.

SECRET LANGUAGE SCHOOL

How did linguists secretly trained at Fort Snelling help shorten WWII by two years and save the lives of thousands of American soldiers?

Fort Snelling was constructed in 1820 as a military outpost at the confluence of the Mississippi and Minnesota rivers (also known as Bdote, see "Where the Waters Meet," page 58). It's now a National Historic Landmark where people can connect to both proud and somber stories of those who crossed paths there over the centuries: stories of soldiers and veterans, Native peoples, enslaved people, immigrants, and the changing landscape. One story involves a classified Japanese language school housed at the fort during World War II. Its impact on war efforts was profound.

In the early 1940s, US military leaders recognized the need for battle-ready translators proficient in the Japanese language, so they established a school to train second-generation Japanese Americans (Nisei) at the Presidio in San Francisco. But then in February 1942, two months after the Japanese military attacked Pearl Harbor, President Franklin D. Roosevelt issued Executive Order 9066. This document forced 112,000 Japanese Americans living on the West Coast into prison camps due to a perceived threat.

Needing to relocate inland, the language school's commander, Colonel Kai Rasmussen, found a new home when Minnesota Governor Harold Stassen welcomed the school

---

The linguists played a key role in shortening WWII by translating captured documents, interrogating prisoners of war, and interpreting enemy orders and commands.

With a human history that goes back ten thousand years, Fort Snelling and the historic landscape surrounding it evoke complex emotions. A current revitalization project focuses on richer, fuller stories—including the darker or more secretive ones—of the people who lived, died, and crossed paths there.

to Camp Savage and later Fort Snelling. Renamed the Military Intelligence Service Language School (MISLS), the school graduated over six thousand linguists. Many of them were volunteers from the prison camps who served while their families were still incarcerated.

FORT SNELLING AND FORMER MILITARY INTELLIGENCE SERVICE LANGUAGE SCHOOL

WHAT Impact of battle-ready translators trained at the fort during WWII

WHERE 200 Tower Ave., Saint Paul

COST Admission, $6–$12

PRO TIP Learn more about the fort's revitalization project underway at mnhs.org/fortsnelling.

Graduates from the school accompanied combat troops in every major landing in the Pacific for both the United States and allied forces. They also acted as interpreters at war crime trials and served under General Douglas MacArthur's occupation force in Japan. The Nisei linguists are credited with shortening World War II in the Pacific theater by two years, saving the lives of thousands of American soldiers and billions in American dollars.

THE *MARY TYLER MOORE* "EXTRA"

Who was the befuddled-looking woman in the background during MTM's famous hat toss?

Everyone knows who can turn the world on with her smile—Mary Richards on *The Mary Tyler Moore Show*, of course—that spunky thirty-something who came to Minneapolis to make a fresh start by working as an associate producer for fictional television station WJM. A cultural touchstone, the 1970s sitcom was actually filmed in Los Angeles but featured Minneapolis landmarks and amenities in the opening credits, such as Lake of the Isles and the IDS Crystal Court. The show polished Minneapolis's image and inspired young, career-minded women for generations.

The opening montage changed over the years, but the final hat toss was a constant. That scene was filmed in 1969 on a cold January day in downtown Minneapolis. At the same time, a woman by the name of Hazel Frederick—wearing a green coat, fur collar, and a scarf over her head—happened to be exiting the revolving doors of the now defunct Donaldson's Department Store. Suddenly, an attractive brunette in front of her stopped and gleefully threw her hat in the air. Frederick, looking a little perplexed, became an unknowing extra in one of the greatest show openings in the history of television, now memorialized in bronze at Seventh Street and Nicollet Mall.

"I didn't even know what was going on. I just walked up to this crowd and this woman threw her hat up in the air. I guess I just got in the way." —Hazel Frederick (Source: *Star Tribune*, October 19, 1996.)

Hazel Frederick, the woman with a scarf over her head, never earned a dime from her cameo in the opening montage of The Mary Tyler Moore Show. *Bonus Trivia: The beret that Mary tossed in downtown Minneapolis was a gift from Mary's aunt and was sadly stolen from Mary's attic years later.*

MARY TYLER MOORE'S HAT TOSS SCENE

WHAT The story behind the sitcom's iconic hat toss including Hazel, the puzzled-looking woman in the background

WHERE MTM hat toss statue, 700 Nicollet Mall, Minneapolis

COST Free

PRO TIP Another photo op is the exterior of Mary's old bachelorette pad in the three-story Victorian at 2104 Kenwood Parkway (but keep in mind that real people live there, so stay on the sidewalk).

Hazel's identity remained largely unknown until 1996, when she and Mary met for the first time at a Mall of America book signing for Mary's autobiography, *After All*. Moore invited Frederick on stage and introduced her as "my costar." According to Frederick's obituary, she was born in 1908 and died in 1999. From the late 1950s to the mid-1960s, she worked at the Minnesota State Sanatorium for Consumptives near Walker. After her husband's death in 1966, she moved to Minneapolis and worked at the Glen Lake Sanatorium until she retired.

ONE, TWO, UP SHE GOES!

What is the Twin Cities' oldest and highest-flying parade attraction?

From the free candy to the decorated trucks, people across America love parades. In the Twin Cities, there's a parade attraction unlike anywhere else—the Saint Paul Bouncing Team. Its one-of-a-kind blanket tosses, which date back to the first Saint Paul Winter Carnival in 1886, have been captivating local parade goers for more than 130 years. And according to team members, it's the only group like it in the world.

The concept was inspired by an old hunting tradition in which a clan member would get tossed into the air from an animal skin to better see their prey across the tundra. In contrast, the bouncing team tosses a female acrobat, called "the bouncing girl," from a canvas blanket to amaze a crowd.

Fourteen "pullers" hold onto straps attached around the blanket. Then they pull at exactly the same time after chanting "One, two, up she goes!" Except when they perform at the Cinco de Mayo Parade in West Side Saint Paul. Then, of course, it's "Uno, dos, arriba!" When the bouncing girl reaches twenty to thirty-five feet in the air, she waves and flips, twists, or toe-touch straddles before plopping back onto the blanket.

Bouncing girls are selected during annual tryouts inside Landmark Center. They range in age from twenty-one to sixty-two and are incredible athletes who often have backgrounds in gymnastics, diving, cheerleading, or ice skating. Although the group is best known for its Saint Paul Winter Carnival

---

In the early 1970s, one of the Saint Paul Bouncing Girls, while in the air, waved to US President Nixon, who happened to be walking through one of the city skyways.

The Saint Paul Bouncing Team made its debut more than a century ago at the very first Winter Carnival. It's now a nonprofit organization, supported by its members, who appear at several parades and events throughout the year. Photos courtesy of the Saint Paul Bouncing Team.

appearances, it performs at a variety of local parades and events year-round. A calendar of events is listed on its website. They've even bounced a few celebrities over the years, including former governor Jesse Ventura, comedian Steve Allen, longtime NBC weatherman Willard Scott, NFL All-Pro center Matt Birk, and Santa Claus.

SAINT PAUL BOUNCING TEAM

WHAT Longtime blanket tossing/ parade tradition

WHERE Appearance schedule is posted at stpaulbouncingteam.org

COST Donations are accepted on the website

PRO TIP Locals, they're always looking for new enthusiastic, friendly team members with strong arms and backs to serve as pullers.

SKY-RISES FOR BEES

Where can bees pollinate in a room with a view?

Millions of people live in sky-rises around the world. And in the Twin Cities, so do some bees. Due to habitat loss, pesticide contamination, and climate change, native bees depended on for ecosystem stability are spiraling toward extinction. In response, the University of Minnesota Bee Lab and Public Art Saint Paul joined forces to create the "Pollinator Sky Rise"—a groundbreaking combination of sculpture and science. It's the first of its kind in the world. Saint Paul is home to three of them, installed in the Como and Phalen neighborhoods. There is also one outside the University of Minnesota Weisman Art Museum in Minneapolis.

Each structure—roughly four feet by three feet and elevated on a pole—is a quirky, geometric cluster of "studio apartments" (bee houses) made of wood and steel. The bees choose a hole they like. Then the mother bee builds walls using materials like resin and leaves to create little rooms, which she stocks with nectar and pollen for offspring.

The immature bees live in the holes during the harsh winter. Researchers monitor activity to discover what kind of man-made housing will attract, protect, and nurture pollinators at a time when natural habitat is disappearing. The structures are designed to attract native, solitary stem-nesting bees such as mason bees and stem-cutting bees. After the research project ends, the dwellings will remain in place as public art.

The sky-rises attract the kind of wild bees that live in decaying material such as dead branches, which are frequently discarded in urban environments.

Bright, geometric, and quirky sky-rises for bees are stellar examples of how city artists use their skills to address social issues.

"POLLINATOR SKY RISE" DWELLINGS FOR BEES

WHAT A series of high-rise habitats designed to attract and protect wild bees under threat due to habitat loss

WHERE Find locations at publicartstpaul.org

COST Free

PRO TIP See beelab.umn.edu to learn about a wide range of local bee initiatives.

The sky-rises, part of a larger local initiative called Bee Real Bee Everywhere, were created by the artistic team of Christine Baeumler, Amanda Lovelee, and Julie Benda. As part of Bee Real Bee Everywhere, bee enthusiasts ride through town on a custom-made cargo bike, which they call their Office of Urban Pollen Exchange. They distribute seed packets at parks, libraries, and farmers markets while encouraging individuals to grow their own pollinator gardens.

LUTEFISK HOTLINE

What exactly is lutefisk, and who can you call to ensure yours doesn't end up looking like fish Jell-O?

Scandinavian roots run deep in Minnesota. Due to overpopulation and poor farming conditions in their homelands, hundreds of thousands of Swedish and Norwegian immigrants settled in the state between 1851 and 1920. Their presence has led to the widespread nature of Lutheranism, hotdish, Vikings "Skol" chants, Sven and Ole jokes, long o's, polite reserve, and, of course, lutefisk—the piece of cod "that passeth all understanding."

Madison, in southwestern Minnesota, touts itself as the nation's lutefisk capital. But Minneapolis is home to one of the world's highest-volume lutefisk processors—Olsen Fish Company. Ya, you betcha. It even offers a Lutefisk Hotline (1-800-882-0212). You'll find the number printed on napkins and placemats in church basements throughout the land.

The Olsen Fish Company has been operating on the Northside of Minneapolis since 1910, when it was founded by Olaf Frederick Olsen and John W. Norberg. Not surprisingly, sales are dropping because the younger generation is losing its ancestral traditions. Still, the company sells more than a few hundred thousand pounds of lutefisk a year. Soaked in water and lye (which is basically an FDA-approved version of drain cleaner) for days, it's considered a nostalgic delicacy to some and a quivering glob to others. Most would agree that eating it once a year is probably enough.

OLSEN FISH COMPANY

WHAT One of the world's highest-volume lutefisk processors

WHERE 2115 N. Second St., Minneapolis

COST $7–$9 per pound at retailers throughout North America

PRO TIP When cooking lutefisk, the fork test is important. It should slide right off the fork, according to the Olsen Fish Company Lutefisk Hotline.

Shown here is a tub of six hundred pounds of soaking lutefisk at Olsen Fish Company, which has been hand-packing fresh-to-order lutefisk since 1910.

Olsen Fish Company products can be found at retailers throughout North America. Around the holidays, the line to buy its lutefisk products sold at Ingebretsen's, the long-standing Scandinavian store on Lake Street, goes out the door. To lure millennials, Olsen Fish Company is considering someday offering prepared foods such as bacon-wrapped lutefisk or lutefisk tacos. It tried selling lutefisk TV dinners a few years back, but that didn't go over so well.

"Every Advent we entered the purgatory of lutefisk, a repulsive gelatinous fishlike dish that tasted of soap and gave off an odor that would gag a goat," wrote Minnesota's Garrison Keillor in his book *Lake Wobegon Days*.

SIXTY-ACRE SCULPTURE

Where did a college professor mold and sculpt his gigantic backyard into a public art park?

Many parks are used as backdrops for sculptures. But Caponi Art Park, all sixty acres of it, is itself a sculpture. It all started when the late Anthony Caponi—an Italian-American artist, philosopher, innovator, and longtime Macalester College art professor—purchased the vast wooded area hidden off Diffley Road in Eagan in 1949. First, he built a house, where he eventually raised a family of six children. Then, he began transforming his rugged backyard into a public art park, which he often referred to as his "sixty-acre sculpture."

For decades, Caponi, along with his wife, Cheryl, used a shovel, wheelbarrow, and his Bobcat to carve out his magical woodland. It's like a giant bowl with hundreds of trees, miles of trails, curvy stone walls, and stone and metal artwork scattered throughout. Since the artwork is blended into nature, you may miss it if you're not paying attention.

Look for the giant snake built into a small mossy hillside. And images of people huddled together molded into a retaining wall, representing the victims of the volcanic eruption that buried the ancient Roman city of Pompeii. Look for sculptures here and there of birds and sisters and mothers and daughters and lovers. One sculpture features caveman forms on one side and Einstein's equation and Beethoven's musical notes on the

Anthony Caponi, who passed away in 2015, designed the park as a place for people to experience art in natural surroundings. Rather than intrude upon nature, he incorporated it by molding earth into art walls and cascading slopes into sculptures.

Consistent with the philosophy of the park to blend nature and art, the favorite giant beast sculpture featuring the head of a rattlesnake and the body of an anaconda is an integral part of the small hill that supports the art studio next to it.

other, depicting the intellectual progression of humankind.

In 1992, the park was incorporated as a nonprofit to preserve and enhance Caponi's vision with arts and education programming. On the north side, accessed from the parking lot through a pedestrian tunnel under Diffley Road, is the Sculpture Garden. It features about thirty pieces, but it may feel sparse until you take a closer look. On the south side of Diffley Road rests the park's amphitheater nestled into the hilly landscape beneath a canopy of trees. The Theater in the Woods, as it's called, is a unique setting for theatrical, literary, and musical performances for the whole family.

CAPONI ART PARK

WHAT Art park with sixty acres of rolling, wooded hills embedded with art

WHERE 1220 Diffley Rd., Eagan

COST Free self-guided tours and performances; donations appreciated. Guided walking tours $4 per person. Guided golf cart tours $40 - $50, depending on group size.

PRO TIP Check website for program information. Closed on Mondays and in the winter. To better appreciate the offbeat and sparse-feeling Sculpture Garden, download a park guide for a map and artwork descriptions.

THE FORTY-FIFTH PARALLEL

Where in the Twin Cities can you stand halfway between the equator and the North Pole?

As we all learned in geography class, our world is marked with a grid of invisible lines—longitude and latitude—to help us locate any point on earth. Did you know the forty-fifth degree of latitude north, also known as the forty-fifth parallel, which marks the halfway point between the equator and the North Pole, runs through the Twin Cities?

It first enters the western suburbs, passing through Medicine Lake, Golden Valley, and North Minneapolis before it crosses the Mississippi into Northeast Minneapolis, then Roseville and Lake Elmo. From there, it makes its way across the St. Croix into Wisconsin, then around the world and back again. Local writer and artist Andy Sturdevant once wrote an especially detailed column in *MinnPost* that mentions certain Twin Cities streets and businesses the parallel line runs through, such as the Salvation Army on Lyndale Avenue North and the Maplewood Moose Lodge.

The forty-fifth parallel in the Twin Cities is officially marked in three places. One of the markers is a stone slab placed in the grass along the Roseville Heritage Trail. It's located slightly north of the corner of Cleveland and Roselawn avenues.

"The least Minneapolis can do to honor the forty-fifth parallel of north latitude for its long residence here is to designate its course with appropriate tablets." (Source: *Minneapolis Tribune*, October 6, 1916, via mnmuseumofthems.org.)

Across the street from a directional sign at the intersection of Golden Valley Road and Theodore Wirth Parkway (which also points the way to Wirth Parkway's awesome snow tubing hill) lies a boulder with one of the forty-fifth parallel markers on it. You'll find it in the middle of a small triangle of grassy park land next to a dead-end sign.

Another is a sign along the pathway around Medicine Lake in Plymouth. And the other is mounted on a boulder located in the middle of a small grassy triangle at the intersection of Theodore Wirth Parkway and Golden Valley Road in the suburb of Golden Valley. The Golden Valley marker was placed by the Minneapolis Park Board in the fall of 1916, making it the second-oldest forty-fifth parallel marker in the nation (although it was updated at some point).

HALFWAY POINT BETWEEN EQUATOR AND NORTH POLE

WHAT An invisible line that passes through the Twin Cities, marking the halfway point between the equator and the North Pole

WHERE Markers in Golden Valley, Roseville, and at Medicine Lake. More details in the story.

COST Free

PRO TIP The forty-fifth parallel is an east and west line that is exactly one-half the distance between the equator and the North Pole or a distance of 3,102 miles each way, according to the information on the stone slab at the Roseville forty-fifth parallel marker.

MAGIC OF SKYROCK

Where is there an astonishing collection of European dance organs and miniature merry-go-rounds inside a farmhouse?

Twenty minutes west of Minneapolis, on a winding country road, you'll find an extraordinary place. Skyrock Farm is a premier horse-training facility where you can enjoy lush gardens, the excitement of high-jumping horses, a mini roller coaster, and an awe-inspiring collection of European dance organs and antique carousels tucked inside a soaring farmhouse. When the power switches are turned on and the music starts, it's like standing in the middle of an 1800s street carnival.

At the heart of the collection is a quaint carousel featuring full-size, antique wooden horses (and a zebra) turning round and round to what is referred to as "the happiest music on earth." The wooden horses, each at least a hundred years old and restored by owner Bill Nunn, were created for fairs in Europe. An eclectic mix of circus paraphernalia is also scattered throughout, including a carnival donkey, a gorilla turning side to side, and even a clown doing nonstop push-ups.

Nunn and his wife, Stacy, have been breeding and training jumping horses for over thirty years. About fifteen years ago, they opened their eleven-acre homestead for tours and special events. A typical tour starts in the carousel building, followed by a home-cooked meal in the ballroom. Visitors then have the option of touring the heated horse barn, where they learn about the important roles that horses have played throughout history and enjoy a jumping-horse exhibition.

Owner Bill Nunn even punches out his own organ music on paper rolls. He says it takes three hours to punch out one minute of music!

154

SKYROCK FARM AND CAROUSEL

WHAT Farmhouse featuring extensive collection of circus organs and miniature carousels

WHERE 2825 Willow Dr. N., Medina

COST Tours, by appointment only, $40 with a minimum group size of twenty

PRO TIP Check skyrockcarousel.com for more info on tours and special events. Check skyrockfarm.com for more info on riding lessons and camps.

At first glance, Skyrock Farm looks like any other farm. But there are surprises everywhere, starting with an outdoor mini roller coaster. But wait until you see the collection inside the big building across from the horse barn! Exterior photo courtesy of Amanda Severson.

CITYWIDE BOOK OF POETRY

What's the deal with all the poems stamped on Saint Paul sidewalks?

Sidewalks protect us from traffic, inspire active living, and make neighborhoods more vibrant. Thanks to all the lovely poems stamped into the sidewalks of Saint Paul each year, they also give us beautiful and clever things to read.

In 2008, Marcus Young, then an artist for Public Art Saint Paul, figured since the city's Department of Public Works has to repour ten miles of cracked sidewalks each year anyway, why not stamp something special into them? In the tradition of the Twin Cities' remarkable literary culture, Young worked with the city to begin an annual poetry contest, now called Sidewalk Poetry. It's still going strong.

Saint Paul residents submit short, original poems of three hundred characters or less for a chance to win $100 and have their work "published" on city sidewalks. Locations to pour the winning poems into wet cement are selected from slabs marked for replacement. To date, there have been more than one thousand poems stamped into the sidewalks from a collection that now includes fifty-four individual poems, each one poured in several locations.

Thanks to an award-winning initiative started by a Public Art Saint Paul artist in 2008, everyone who lives or works in Saint Paul is now within a ten-minute walk of a sidewalk poem.

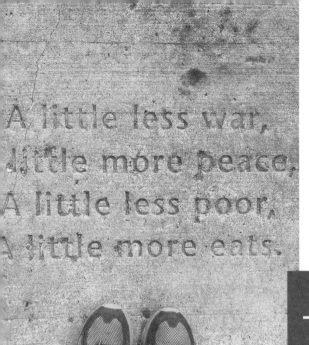

A little less war,
A little more peace,
A little less poor,
A little more eats.

This poem, by Eyang Wu, stamped in a sidewalk on Selby Avenue and other sidewalk locations since 2008, is one of more than one thousand sidewalk poems throughout Saint Paul.

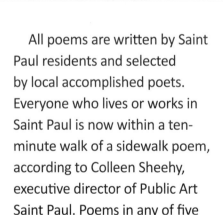

SIDEWALK POETRY

WHAT Poems by Saint Paul residents that are stamped into newly poured sidewalks each year

WHERE Maps with locations can be found at stpaul.gov and publicartstpaul.org.

COST Free

PRO TIP Make a treasure hunt out of finding as many poems as you can in an afternoon. In the process, you'll find all kinds of quaint neighborhood parks and shops you never knew existed before.

All poems are written by Saint Paul residents and selected by local accomplished poets. Everyone who lives or works in Saint Paul is now within a ten-minute walk of a sidewalk poem, according to Colleen Sheehy, executive director of Public Art Saint Paul. Poems in any of five languages—English, Dakota, Hmong, Spanish, and Somali—are accepted to honor the cultures represented throughout the city. For non-English poems, writers are asked to submit a written translation. Saint Paul is the first city to have such an extensive program for sidewalk poetry that is integrated into the city's infrastructure.

INSANE ASYLUM MAKEOVER

Why did choirs of people gather to sing and pray at a former insane asylum?

The phrase "insane asylum" conjures up images of big, spooky gothic institutions. But the one overlooking the Rum River in the town of Anoka was made to feel "like home." Opened in 1900, the Anoka Asylum (later renamed Anoka State Hospital) is where wards of the state lived in large brick cottages around a grassy park for more than a century. Many of them are buried at the on-site cemetery. For a long time, the graves were marked only with numbers, but they all have headstones with names now.

Some say it was one of the most humanely run mental institutions in the country. Others reported mistreatment, including lobotomies and isolation. Of course, attitudes and knowledge about treating mental illness in those days were much different

ANOKA STATE HOSPITAL COTTAGES

WHAT Cottages on the spooky grounds of the old Anoka State Hospital transformed into bright and welcoming housing for war veterans

WHERE 3300 Fourth Ave., Anoka

COST Veterans pay a sliding fee to stay in the cottages, roughly $17 per day.

PRO TIP It's an interesting place to drive around, but entering the buildings is prohibited.

In 1949, on Halloween night, Minnesota's Governor Youngdahl went to the asylum and, using a torch, burned hundreds of restraints and straitjackets in front of a crowd. In a speech, he said the burning "liberated patients from barbarous devices and the approach which these devices symbolized." (Source: AsylumProjects.org.)

Opened in 1900, the Anoka Asylum was created to feel more like home than an institution, with large cottages circling a lovely courtyard. Cottage Two was the first of the three century-old cottages at Anoka State Hospital to get a "miraculous" makeover.

than they are today. Some patients took their own lives while trying to escape in the tunnel system beneath the cottages constructed to transport patients. Not surprisingly, this has led to ghostly lore.

The hospital operated until 1999, when it was moved to a nearby facility. After that, Anoka County used part of the property to house government offices and the county workhouse. Closed and boarded up, the other buildings sat vacant, gathering mold, dust, and graffiti until 2017. In efforts to save the buildings from demolition, the city announced an idea with the theme "Saving Veterans' Lives While Saving Our History."

Hundreds of volunteers began transforming three of the decrepit cottages into transitional housing for veterans. Choirs of people came to sing and pray on each floor to "clear out the darkness." In less than sixty days, the first cottage was completely overhauled. "That's what a whole lot of community can do," said Eagle's Nest founder Melony Butler during a TPT Twin Cities PBS *Almanac* segment. Eagle's Nest led the renovation effort. Haven for Heroes has since taken over.

"OH, GOOD GRIEF!"

What's the story behind the *Peanuts* statues scattered all over Saint Paul?

The Twin Cities area has been home to lots of famous people. But the most infinitely relatable is Charles M. Schulz, who lightened the human condition with his comic strip *Peanuts*. Although he was born in Minneapolis, Schulz grew up in Saint Paul. His father owned a barbershop, which later became the site of the legendary (and now sadly closed) O'Gara's Bar & Grill.

As a boy, Schulz lived in a humble home at 473 Macalester Street, climbed monkey bars at Mattocks Park, and caddied at Highland Golf Course. He graduated from Saint Paul Central High School, where Schulz claimed he was an outcast, routinely flunked classes (and dating), and had his cartoons rejected by the yearbook staff.

After serving in WWII, he moved back to the Twin Cities and taught drawing classes at the Art Instruction School. It was there where he fell head over heels for the school's red-headed accountant, Donna. Schulz proposed. Donna turned him down and married a Minneapolis firefighter instead. She later became the inspiration for the Little Red-Haired Girl character in *Peanuts*. "You never get over your first love," the cartoonist once said.

On February 12, 2000, the night before his final Sunday comic strip was scheduled to appear in newspapers, Schulz died in his sleep from colon cancer at age seventy-seven. Soon after, Saint Paul launched a five-year public art project titled *Peanuts on*

Schulz initially named his strip *Li'l Folks*. But when it was first syndicated in 1950, it was changed to *Peanuts*, a name he detested his entire career because, to him, that word meant "insignificant."

Pictured are just a few of the several hundred Peanuts *statues created in the early 2000s.* Charlie Brown Gets on Bass, *designed by Ann Dickinson and M. Moline;* Sweeten Up Lucy, *designed by David Brown and Pam Ruiz; and gangster* Babyface Snoopy, *designed by Anne Emily Heaney.*

Parade, a series of five-foot-tall *Peanuts* statues, each vibrantly painted by a different artist. Santa Rosa, California, where Schulz lived in the latter part of his life, picked up the tradition for another four years. In the end, there were eight hundred statues. Many were auctioned off to help fund scholarships and permanent bronze sculptures in Saint Paul and Santa Rosa. But well over a hundred of them can still be seen on public display throughout Saint Paul.

CHARLES SCHULZ AND THE *PEANUTS* STATUES

WHAT The local mastermind behind the *Peanuts* gang and a series of statues dedicated to him

WHERE Locations of the statues can be found in *The Complete History of Peanuts on Parade* Vol. 1, featuring in-depth stories by William Johnson.

COST Free

PRO TIP Check out the statues in front of Candyland on Wabasha Street as an excuse to load up on homemade fudge.

FOSSIL FIX

Where can you satisfy your dinosaur fossil fix?

The Twin Cities area isn't exactly a hotbed for dinosaur fossils. In fact, to date, there have been only three remnants found in all of Minnesota: a serrated tooth, a chunk of vertebrae, and most recently a ninety-million-year-old claw bone most likely belonging to a two-legged velociraptor.

One reason for a lack of fossils may be that they eroded from glaciers that raked through the state. Of course, you can always satisfy your fossil fix by visiting the Science Museum of Minnesota, which features one of the most complete Triceratops skeletons in the world. But you can also head over to ZRS Fossils in South Minneapolis. It's a good place to satisfy your crystal cravings too.

Owned and operated by Kelly Lund and John McArdle, ZRS Fossils offers a huge variety of earth's treasures. The first thing you'll notice is not a dinosaur fossil but a seventy-thousand-year-old, eight-foot-tall cave bear skeleton named Boris, found in Russia. Boris is not for sale, but everything else in the store is.

ZRS FOSSILS AND GIFTS

WHAT Shop featuring fossils and other unique treasures of the earth

WHERE 3018 Lyndale Ave. S., Minneapolis

COST Items available for all budgets

PRO TIP If you're a die-hard dinosaur lover with a sweet tooth, pay a visit to T-Rex, a cookie shop in Eagan that features five-pound cookies!

ZRS Fossils is bursting at the seams with unique treasures from the earth, from authentic dinosaur fossils to an exquisite collection of minerals, gems, and natural stone carvings.

The first thing you'll notice at ZRS Fossils is not a dinosaur fossil but a seventy-thousand-year-old cave bear, named Boris, found in the Ural Mountains of Russia. But keep looking, and you'll find a wealth of dinosaur remnants mixed in with cases loaded with crystals.

In the market for an oviraptor egg nest? A giant mosasaur tooth? Gizzard stones? Sterling silver jewelry made from dinosaur bones? For just a few dollars, you can get yourself a fossilized cephalopod from the Devonian period (350 million years ago). If prehistoric critters aren't your thing, there are glass cases packed with shiny minerals and beautifully crafted carvings from as far away as Morocco.

ZRS also offers mineral- and fossil-hunting field trips around the country. Led by paleontologists, they provide hands-on learning experiences for all ages. You get to keep what you find. Avid collectors and travel enthusiasts would love the annual GeoTour adventures to collect fossils, agates, and crystals in Morocco, Australia, and England. Plus, on-site lapidary classes offer patrons opportunities to learn how to transform minerals and fossils into jewelry.

SEMINARY SURPRISE

Why have generations of Norwegian royalty visited a little log church tucked up on a hill in Saint Paul?

Hidden amidst the pine trees overlooking Luther Seminary in Saint Paul is a little log building dripping wi th history. Known as Old Muskego Church, it was constructed in 1844 and is the first Norwegian Lutheran house of worship in America. It was originally constructed in southeastern Wisconsin by Norwegian immigrants who had settled in Muskego, Wisconsin.

After twenty-five years of serving a congregation of nearly three hundred members, the church became too small for the soaring Norwegian population. The building was then sold to a farmer who used it briefly as a barn. In 1904, it was purchased by the United Norwegian Lutheran Church in America. Then it was relocated to Luther Seminary in Saint Paul after being taken apart and reassembled log by log.

During its years on campus, the church has been mainly used for festival services and small weddings. It has also been used

Built in 1844 by Norwegian immigrants, the hidden Norse treasure is tucked away behind the library and up a slight hill on the campus of Luther Seminary in Saint Paul.

Old Muskego Church was moved, log by log, from the Muskego settlement in Wisconsin to the campus of Luther Seminary in 1904. Its years of service have ensured that the legacy of America's Norwegian settlers will not be forgotten.

as a gathering place for generations of visiting dignitaries, like the king and queen of Norway. As you enter through the front door, you're transported back in time by creaky floors, oak logs, and walnut furnishings. On the main floor, there are fourteen rows of pews, an altar with steps leading up to a pulpit, and a wood-burning stove. Additional seating used to be available in the balcony, but that section is now blocked for safety due to the old and fragile foundation. The building was added to the list of Minnesota State Historical Sites in 1935 and placed on the National Register of Historic Places in 1974.

MOUND BUILDERS

Where was an ancient skull of a child, covered with a red clay mask, found?

It's well known that long before the first European settlers set foot in Minnesota in the 1600s, Native American people inhabited the region. Their historic footprint can be found throughout the state. One deeply interesting place is at Indian Mounds Regional Park, located high atop 450 million-year-old limestone and sandstone bluffs overlooking downtown Saint Paul.

Amongst the park's beautiful city views are six Indian burial mounds. Many scholars believe they were first constructed fifteen hundred to two thousand years ago by Native American people with at least some connection to the ancient Hopewellian culture. But there are still many unanswered questions about their origin and significance.

There used to be dozens of mounds in two separate areas along the bluff. Due to development, however, they were razed, and only six remain. At least seventeen of the original mounds were excavated by looters, road workers, and investigators in the 1880s. Inside, they found bear teeth, copper ornaments, axes, pipes, utensils, mussel shells, pottery embellished with carved animals, and the remains of approximately fifty people, including a few children. The skull of one child was covered with a red clay mask, producing the image of the original face.

"The size, contents, and location of the mounds suggest that they held great religious or ceremonial importance for their builders." (Source: Nelson, Paul. "Indian Mounds Park," *MNopedia*, Minnesota Historical Society.)

It's easy to drive by or below Indian Mounds Regional Park, situated above I-94 in Saint Paul's East Side neighborhood, without stopping to appreciate it. Earlier generations used these mounds—deemed sacred, particularly by the Dakota people—for climbing, picnicking, even ski jumping. Today, they are surrounded by iron fencing to prevent intrusion.

According to a *MNopedia* article published by the Minnesota Historical Society on July 27, 2016, some of the objects and remains taken from the mounds were destroyed in a fire at the State Capitol in 1881. Others were stolen from Macalester College. The same article reports that the only known surviving artifacts from the Saint Paul mounds include seventeen projectile points, a small earthenware vessel, a box of small shells, and a glass bottle of red ocher.

INDIAN MOUNDS REGIONAL PARK

WHAT Public park featuring six prehistoric Native American burial mounds

WHERE 10 Mounds Blvd. N., Saint Paul

COST Free

PRO TIP New to the park is a mile-long tree trek that you can stroll along and visit twenty-eight unique trees, all marked with a small information post.

NORTHWEST NOSTALGIA

Where is the original Northwest Airlines gong?

The legendary story of Northwest Airlines—founded in Minnesota in 1926—is one of highs and lows. Although it was absorbed by Delta in 2008, its colorful history lives on inside a little-known, volunteer-run museum called the Northwest Airlines History Center in Bloomington.

The thirteen-hundred-square-foot room is located inside the Crowne Plaza AiRE MSP Airport hotel across from the fitness center. Featured are thousands of artifacts, including donated photos, model planes, uniforms, airplane seats, a 747 flight-training machine, and of course, a gong!

Some may remember the popular commercials for Northwest featuring Buster Keaton hitting a gong with a polo mallet. The original gong is thought to be somewhere in the Twin Cities. "But nobody seems to know where," said Bruce Kitt, the museum's executive director. Museum visitors can still take a swing (well, a gentle tap) at a cool gong, though. It's one that was gifted to the airline in 1952 during a trade show in Honolulu. The nonprofit museum also has a vast archive located at Flying Cloud Airport in Eden Prairie.

With humble beginnings as a Midwest mail carrier, Northwest became a global leader in air travel. The airline introduced the nation's first closed-cabin commercial plane in 1926, offered nonstop passenger service to "the Orient," and was the first

"In July 1927, Northwest's first passenger flight took off for Chicago. A one-way ticket cost $40, which would be nearly $500 today. The flight took 12.5 hours, including stops in La Crosse, Madison, and Milwaukee." (Source: *The Current*, October 30, 2008.)

Rumor has it that the original Northwest Airlines gong is somewhere in the Twin Cities. Nobody seems to know where, though. A different gong on display at the little-known Northwest Airlines History Center is pretty cool too.

NORTHWEST AIRLINES HISTORY CENTER

WHAT Little-known museum featuring history of Northwest Airlines

WHERE Third floor of the Crowne Plaza AiRE MSP Airport Hotel, 3 Appletree Sq., Bloomington

COST Free

PRO TIP The entire hotel is like an aviation museum. Take a look around at the numerous flight and space technology photographs throughout the hallways and grab a bite at the on-site AiRECraft Grill. Before you go to the museum, call first to ensure it'll be open.

major airline to install oxygen masks and ban smoking.

But it had its failings. For starters, employee policies required flight attendants to undergo girdle checks and sign weight contracts. To be fair, that was the industry norm back then. Another blunder was the time NWA handed out a money-saving tip sheet to laid-off employees, which included taking shorter showers and rummaging through other people's trash. Even so, there is a deep sense of nostalgia for the airline that, in its golden years, provided extraordinary service, technological leadership, and well-paying jobs for tens of thousands of Minnesotans.

EIGHTY-ONE MINUTES

Where is there an award-winning tribute to the I-35W bridge collapse rescue efforts?

Twin Citians will never forget August 1, 2007. It was the height of the evening rush hour. The Interstate 35W bridge in Minneapolis was filled with traffic, slowed to a crawl by road construction. With no warning, it collapsed and plunged into the dark waters of the Mississippi.

Eighty-four cars and more than two hundred people went down with it. A school bus filled with kids hovered on the edge. While miraculous survivor stories abound, thirteen people were killed and 144 were injured. Five years later, the extraordinary rescue efforts were memorialized in an exhibit permanently on display inside the Firefighters Hall & Museum, a hidden treasure of Northeast Minneapolis with artifacts highlighting local heroism dating back to the 1860s.

Titled *Eighty-One Minutes: After the Bridge Collapsed*, the exhibit chronicles in great detail the efficient rescue efforts in the immediate aftermath, from the first dispatch call to the last victim cleared. Sifting through water and dangerously moving concrete, first responders rescued all survivors from the scene in eighty-one minutes. SALA Architects worked with Minneapolis firefighters and Bluestem Heritage over a series of months to create the display. It features steel and disorienting angles to reflect the collapse site. The exhibit has since been

---

The *Eighty-One Minutes* exhibit features steel and disorienting angles to reflect the horrific bridge collapse. At the entrance is the sign that hung by the I-35W bridge at the time. The sign is a loan from the Minnesota Historical Society.

Gain insight into the extraordinary rescue efforts that took place immediately following the I-35W bridge collapse by viewing a display tucked inside the Firefighters Hall & Museum in Northeast Minneapolis.

cited for an award of merit by the American Association for State and Local History.

Within a few days of the collapse, the Minnesota Department of Transportation began planning a replacement bridge—the I-35W St. Anthony Falls Bridge. Construction was completed rapidly, and it opened on September 18, 2008. Located near Gold Medal Park on West River Parkway Trail is the I-35W Bridge Memorial Remembrance Garden. It consists of a survivor's wall and thirteen steel columns, one for each person who died.

EIGHTY-ONE MINUTES: AFTER THE BRIDGE COLLAPSED

WHAT A permanent exhibit that documents the heroic response to the I-35W bridge collapse

WHERE Firefighters Hall & Museum: 664 Twenty-Second Ave. NE, Minneapolis

COST Adults, $8; children ages 3–12, $5

PRO TIP Open Saturdays only. The museum, which is available for group tours and birthday parties, appeals to kids, too, with a fire pole to slide down and trucks to sit in.

TIED UP IN KNOTS

Which Saint Paul invention was saved by *The Tonight Show*? And what is the inventor up to these days?

Post-it Notes. Rollerblades. Handled grocery bags. Retractable safety belts. Tonka Trucks. Organ transplants. Scotch tape. Bisquick. The implantable pacemaker. The Bundt pan. The pop-up toaster. The list of groundbreaking inventions born in the Twin Cities goes on and on. Each has its own story of innovation and perseverance. The one tangled in the most "scandal," though, was perhaps Twister—one of America's most iconic games. It all started in 1965 when Saint Paul native Reyn Guyer, co-owner of his dad's design company at the time, created a shoe polish promotion. It involved a polka dot paper mat.

   With a knack for product development, Guyer suddenly imagined the mat as a floor game utilizing real people as playing pieces. Local artist Charles Foley and toy designer Neil Rabens helped him develop the game further. They organized the colored circles in rows, added the spinner, suggested players use hands as well as feet, and named it Pretzel. The rights were sold to Milton Bradley Company, which renamed it Twister. The game made some executives feel a little uneasy, though.

A few years after he created Twister, Saint Paul native Reyn Guyer created the Nerf Ball. His more recent endeavors include a dice game called Rally Roll and a lawn game called King's Court. He also co-founded Wrensong Entertainment, an independent music company, and Winsor Learning, a reading intervention program in Bloomington.

Twister sales exploded after Johnny Carson and Eva Gabor played it in front of millions on The Tonight Show *on May 3, 1966. Originally called Pretzel, Twister was inducted into the National Toy Hall of Fame in 2015.*

THE STORY OF TWISTER

WHAT The iconic game born from a Saint Paul ad man

WHERE In stores everywhere, of course

COST Varies

PRO TIP Check out *MN Invents*, a collection of books documenting "the secret and ongoing history of the great Minnesota inventive culture."

Although the game's intention was innocent enough, the idea of a board game requiring such close contact was considered socially questionable for the times. When Sears, Roebuck and Company—then one of the nation's most dominant retailers—refused to include it in its family-friendly catalog, production stopped.

But on May 3, 1966, Johnny Carson played it with his guest, Eva Gabor, on *The Tonight Show*. The audience was in hysterics. The next day, the one New York store that stocked the game that "ties you up in knots" sold out to a line of customers. In response, Milton Bradley (now Hasbro) resumed production. Sears changed its mind. Sales exploded. And Twister has been a hit for all ages ever since.

SKYWAY SCOOP

How did skyways get their start, and where is the oldest?

Minneapolis has the world's most extensive skyway network, but Saint Paul can claim the *oldest* skyway structure. It's tucked between the two towers of the First National Bank Building, known for the red neon "1st" on top of it. According to the building's general manager, the copper-clad passageway with six tinted windows built in 1931 is "the oldest skyway in the Midwest, if not the country." Also the metro's highest skyway, it looks like a strangely wedged Lego from the street.

Overall, though, the idea for elevated, enclosed walkways took root in the mid-1950s in Minneapolis. By that time, General Mills and other major employers had abandoned downtown for the suburbs. Then along came Southdale—the nation's first fully enclosed shopping mall. City leaders knew something had to be done to lure shoppers back downtown.

In 1962, ribbons were cut for the Twin Cities' first all-weather pedestrian skyway spanning Seventh Street between Marquette and Second avenues, which has since been demolished. But it was the construction of the IDS Center in 1974 with skyways stretching in all four directions that really got things rolling.

Some believe the glass cocoons have sucked the life off the streets. Some view them as a godsend, allowing downtown workers and visitors to do a thousand different things without having to step out into the frigid, sloshy outdoors. And

---

The Minneapolis Skyway System is the largest continuous system in the world, now connecting eighty blocks spanning nine and a half miles. Saint Paul's Skyway System connects forty-seven blocks spanning five miles.

This tiny old Saint Paul skyway, often touted as the first modern skyway, was built in 1931 to connect the sixteenth floor of the former Merchants Bank Building to the seventeenth floor of the First National Bank Building.

TWIN CITIES SKYWAYS

WHAT The oldest skyway and other lowdown on Minneapolis and Saint Paul skyways

WHERE The oldest: First National Bank Building at 332 Minnesota St., Saint Paul

COST Free

PRO TIP Online skyway maps are available at stpaul.gov and minneapolis.org.

other folks have turned them into floating art galleries. In Minneapolis, just before the skyway entrance to the Wells Fargo East Town towers near US Bank Stadium, is a mural featuring large black-and-white aerial images of downtown through the decades. In Saint Paul, dozens of huge photos of first-generation immigrants have turned four skyways at Sixth and Minnesota streets into memory-tinted light boxes.

DAYTON'S MONKEY AND MEMENTOS

What are the plans for the monkey that was found mummified in the rafters of the legendary department store?

The Minneapolis Dayton's Department Store, built in 1902 on Nicollet Mall by George Draper Dayton, was a magical place. From the candy kitchen and famed Oval Room to the window displays and Daisy Sales, it represented a one-of-a-kind shopping experience for generations of Minnesotans. Even after its name changed to Marshall Field's and then to Macy's, die-hard locals still called it Dayton's.

In 2017, the grand old building closed after 115 years to make way for a new retail complex called The Dayton's Project. During renovations, some interesting items were discovered: Easter eggs, watches, shoes, 1970s Vikings tickets, a fifty-three-year-old wallet (which was returned to its owner). But the biggest surprise of all was a mummified monkey stuck in an air duct. Experts believe it was a 1960s squirrel monkey that likely died after being hit by a fan blade. The warm air then dried and preserved its flesh. But how did it get there?

The most popular theory involves two mischievous teenagers, Larry and Tom. Apparently, one day in 1962, they snuck into the exotic pet shop once housed in the department store and took

According to a Fox News report, a demolition worker for the Dayton's Project submitted a photo of the mummified monkey found stuck in an air duct to the "Old Minneapolis" Facebook page in efforts to find out how it might've gotten there. Immediately, theories began to circulate.

The former Dayton's department store was added to the National Register of Historic Places in 2019. On August 29, 2019, its iconic sign was returned to the building for a new retail and office complex called The Dayton's Project, committed to honoring the store's legacy.

THE DAYTON'S PROJECT AND ITS INTERESTING DISCOVERIES

WHAT Dayton's nostalgia and surprising finds while renovating the legendary department store into a new retail complex

WHERE The Dayton's Project, 700 Nicollet Mall, Minneapolis

COST Free

PRO TIP Keep your eyes open for glimpses of the past while visiting The Dayton's Project. At some point, you might also get glimpses of the surprising items found during renovations, according to Telos Group, LLC, the project's lead developer.

off with a monkey by hiding it inside one of their shirts. A couple of days later, they "returned it" by sneaking it back inside a store entrance. Both gentlemen are now deceased. But Tom's family has since posted an old video of him reminiscing about the incident to his grandkids years ago. And Larry's wife also confirmed the tale was true.

After going on display at the Saint Paul Science Museum lobby, the monkey was returned to The Dayton's Project team. The plan is to have the monkey respectfully preserved at the Minnesota Historical Society, possibly for public viewing in the future. It will be in good company. Cinderella, Pinocchio, and Professor Severus Snape from the Dayton's eighth-floor holiday exhibits are stored there too.

WILLY WONKAISH

What's the maker of the Nut Goodie up to these days?

If you're a Minnesota native of a certain age, there's a good chance you grew up eating those crunchy, chewy blobs of maple nougat, real milk chocolate, and roasted peanuts known as Nut Goodies. After all, they're made in your capital city along the Mississippi corridor at Pearson's Candy Company.

Since Pearson's rarely gives tours, though, more than likely the only glimpse you've had inside the 120,000-square-foot factory is through your imagination. (Giant kettles of caramel, bubbling baths of nougat, waterfalls of milk chocolate . . .) Unless, of course, you've worked there or were one of the lucky ones to find a winning code inside your candy wrapper during their Willy Wonkaish promotion several years ago.

P. Edward Pearson dreamed of making the best candy in the world. He chased that dream in 1909 with the creation of a confectionary plant that first

PEARSON'S CANDY COMPANY

WHAT Inside scoop on the legendary Saint Paul confectionery

WHERE 2140 Seventh St. W., Saint Paul

COST Closed to the public, but help yourself to free whiffs from the parking lot

PRO TIP Tin Whiskers Brewing Company, a few miles away, currently offers a Nut Goodie Porter and Salted Nut Roll Ale in collaboration with Pearson's.

Bonus Trivia: Mars, Inc. (the makers of the Milky Way, Snickers, and M&M's) was also founded in the Twin Cities. They've moved their operations to Chicago, but the Mars family has a private mausoleum at Lakewood Cemetery.

Liquid caramel drizzles into a giant, stainless steel drum like a waterfall inside Pearson's factory along the Mississippi corridor. Courtesy of photographer Brian Gens, who somehow got a rare glimpse inside.

opened in Minneapolis. In 1950, operations were moved to Saint Paul. Roughly two hundred employees now produce $50 million in candy each year.

The first product was the Nut Goodie. Next came the Salted Nut Roll. Then Mint Patties, Bit-O-Honey, and Bun Bars (and others that didn't survive, like the Seven Up Bar and Chicken Dinner Bar). A recent addition is a line of trendy chocolates, called 7th Street Confections, which combines dark chocolate and freeze-dried fruit. Be on the lookout for new packaging, shapes, and variations on the iconic treats in the near future.

Pearson's has seen lots of different owners and changes since its founding. But for the foreseeable future, the plan is to keep growing at its current headquarters on West Seventh Street. Some jobs have been automated over the years. But if you're lucky enough to get an inside glimpse, hopefully you'll still see proud local union confectioners plucking out imperfect peanuts and squeezing on finishing swirls.

MUSHROOMS AND MOBSTERS

Why did local caves used for growing mushrooms become a flashy hideout for mobsters?

If someone in your family tree was an American gangster in the early 1900s, chances are they were either in prison or hanging out in Saint Paul. One of the best ways to peek into this history is a tour of the Wabasha Street Caves.

In 1899, a French immigrant named Albert Mouchotte decided that the caves—originally mined for silica—provided the perfect conditions for growing mushrooms. Before long, the cathedral-like caverns became known as Mushroom Valley. Meanwhile, thanks to a seedy deal with the police chief, they also became hooch-drinking havens for hoodlums.

Saint Paul's police chief, John O'Connor, invited the FBI's most-wanted criminals to use his city as a sanctuary. They could roam freely as long as they paid bribes to city officials and kept their shenanigans out of city limits. (Minneapolis was open game.) When the Prohibition Act of 1919 prohibited the manufacture and sale of alcohol, a speakeasy opened in the caves. After Prohibition ended in 1933, Albert's daughter, Josie, and her husband, William Lehmann, transformed three of the caves into a nightclub called Castle Royal. It became a favorite hangout of

---

Due to a seedy deal, Saint Paul became the epicenter of gangster activity. But when the Barker-Karpis gang kidnapped the president of Hamm's Brewing Company and then the heir to the Schmidt Brewing Company, it all began to unravel.

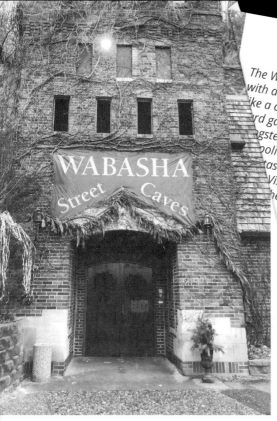

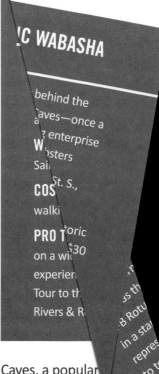

The Wabasha Caves are marked with an ivy-covered facade shaped like a castle. According to legend, a ~~card~~ game in the caves involving four ~~gang~~sters ended in a triple murder. ~~P~~olice mopped up the evidence ~~st~~ashed the bodies under the ~~.~~ Visitors have since reported ~~t~~he men's ghosts float through

C WABASHA

behind the Caves—once a enterprise W sters Sai St. S.,

COS walki

PRO T oric 30 on a wi experier Tour to th Rivers & R

notorious gangsters such as John Dillinger, Ma Barker, and Baby Face Nelson.

Eventually, in the mid-1930s, the O'Connor deal busted up after rampant corruption. Castle Royal closed in 1941. Three decades later, another nightclub named Castle Royal II moved in. The space is now known as the Wabasha Street Caves, a popular weddings, and Thursday Jazz Swing Nights. As for the n business, it flourished in the caves until 1965. After that, William moved it above ground. The business is still in oper Lehmann Farms in Lakeville, Minnesota. You'll find its product local grocery stores and restaurants.

AIRPORT P*TY PRIDE

What's up with a*rt?
bathrooms at M...

Let's be honest...xious. The good news is that
can make us a...International Airport has been doing
Minneapoli...g order, calm, and beauty to the traveler's
whatever ...he bathrooms. The loos are so lovely, in
experier...

...ncy tile mosaics in the

and the mounting security headaches

fact, that in recent years MSP was declared home to America's Best Bathroom in a potty poll by Cintas Corporation, a bathroom product supplier. (The bathrooms at the Varsity Theater in Dinkytown were also once granted that title.)

The most noticeable features are the awe-inspiring, Minnesota-themed tile mosaics that mark the airport bathroom entrances. Each mosaic was created by a different local artist selected from a large pool of applicants. The set of bathrooms that earned MSP the top john award (not shown in photos here) is located on the south end of the Airport Mall in Terminal 1.

MSP A...
BATH...
MO spired by
...es

...lis–Saint
...Airport, 4300
...nneapolis

...o keep your eye out
...inal's floor mosaics,
...e one located in the
...nda. It features a plane
...field and four eagles
...enting the planes lost
...rorists on September 11,
...1.

The women's bathroom features a mosaic with a canoer in the midst of a tranquil tree-lined Minnesota North Shore sunset. The men's bathroom features a mosaic highlighting the state's rich bicycling culture within a calming, blue color scheme.

This tree mosaic on the left titled Seasons of Change *was designed by Barbara Benson Keith and fabricated by Mosaika. It is located in Terminal 1, Concourse E, Gate E8. The floral mosaic on the right named* Minnesota Prairie *was created by Sheryl Tuorila and is located in the North Main Mall of Terminal 1.*

The mosaics in that set were designed by Caron Bell and Mercedes Austin, and the tiles were hand cut, glazed, and baked by Mercury Mosaics, a local artisan clay tile company owned by Austin. As a side note: Mercury Mosaics also has tile work featured in more than one hundred Lululemon stores throughout the country and in local favorites such as The Bachelor Farmer in the Minneapolis North Loop neighborhood.

Each MSP bathroom is used an estimated seven thousand times per day. That's quite an opportunity for local tile artists to share their talents with an ever-changing global audience.

LARGEST RASPBERRY

Why is there a giant raspberry perched on a side street in Hopkins?

Since 1934, the west-metro town of Hopkins has been home to the annual Raspberry Festival, a Twin Cities institution featuring a parade, live music, meat raffles, sporting events, and a golden raspberry hunt. And now it's also home to the world's largest raspberry. The one-thousand-pound cluster of brightly colored drupelets hangs from a twenty-two-foot steel vine near LTD Brewing Company. What's the deal with Hopkins and raspberries anyway?

According to the city's website, Hopkins used to be like a raspberry village, with over eight hundred acres of the super fruit planted at one point. The Raspberry Festival was started to promote sales. Raspberry farming was a lot of work, though. Local children were sent to the fields to pick berries all day long. One woman in the historical account recalls from her childhood picking about four crates' worth a day. That's equal to ninety-six pint-size boxes. Farmers would have to leave home on horses and buggies at 2 a.m. to be at the farmers' market in Minneapolis when it opened at 6 a.m.

By the late 1920s, Hopkins dominated the raspberry scene. In fact, it proclaimed itself the "Raspberry Capital of the World." When the Depression hit, raspberries became a luxury that people could no longer afford. In 1931, a heatwave followed by a drought put many farmers out of business. By the 1960s, the raspberry industry was all but gone from Hopkins. In an effort

---

The largest raspberry in the world, which cost the people of Hopkins $55,000, was unveiled during the town's eighty-third annual Raspberry Festival in 2017.

Created by local artist Ben Janssens at Solid Metal Arts in Northeast Minneapolis, the one-thousand-pound raspberry is dedicated to John Feltl Jr. He is considered the father of Hopkins's famed raspberry industry for developing a method to protect the plants during winter.

WORLD'S LARGEST RASPBERRY

WHAT A tribute to the Hopkins raspberry legacy

WHERE Along Eighth Avenue North in Hopkins (about one block from LTD Brewing Co.)

COST Free

PRO TIP While in town, check out the performance schedule at the long-standing Stages Theatre Company on Main Street.

to "re-raspberry Hopkins," the city has been planting raspberry patches in local parks in recent years. Berry bushes have also been added at the northeast corner of Maetzold Field and by the Depot Coffee Shop on Excelsior Boulevard.

FITZ LAND

Where was F. Scott Fitzgerald born, where did he complete his debut novel, and where did he buy his cigarettes?

Saint Paul is the land of F. Scott Fitzgerald. Born here in 1896, the beloved American writer made his mark all over the city. One can still imagine him and his unpredictable wife, Zelda, arm in arm in their Jazz Age fur coats while walking to sparkling mansion parties in Cathedral Hill. Or while buying cigarettes at W. A. Frost Pharmacy (now a popular restaurant with a really cozy basement). Or while making an entrance at the White Bear Yacht Club, University Club, Saint Paul Hotel, or Commodore.

Dedicated to his life and impact in Saint Paul is a small, elegant nook known as the F. Scott Fitzgerald Reading Alcove located in the George Latimer Central Library, in the Magazine Room on the third floor. One of the things you might learn is that while attending Saint Paul Academy and later Princeton, Fitzgerald struggled academically. Despite his masterful ability to transport readers to champagne garden parties and into the human consciousness, he was a notoriously bad speller. It's thought he suffered from dyslexia.

You'll also surely learn that Fitzgerald and his family bounced around from house to house. One gem is the brick apartment building on Laurel Avenue, where he was born on the second floor. More well known is the brownstone house on Summit Avenue, where he lived with his parents for a short time while

Renowned for such works as *The Great Gatsby*, *Tender Is the Night*, and *This Side of Paradise*, F. Scott Fitzgerald found literary inspiration from around the world, but his true home was Saint Paul.

Francis Scott Key Fitzgerald was born on September 24, 1896, to parents Edward and Mary ("Mollie") McQuillan Fitzgerald in their second-floor apartment of this historically preserved building at 481 Laurel Avenue. The brownstone where he lived with his parents while completing This Side of Paradise *is a half mile away at 599 Summit Avenue.*

completing *This Side of Paradise*, the debut novel that made him an overnight sensation. Fitzgerald left the Midwest in 1922, along with Zelda and their baby girl, for more luxurious destinations. Sadly, Fitzgerald would later sink into alcoholism, while Zelda moved in and out of sanitariums after a mental breakdown.

FITZGERALD IN SAINT PAUL

WHAT Fitzgerald's stomping grounds

WHERE One of the tour stops is Fitzgerald's birthplace: 481 Laurel Ave., Saint Paul.

COST Free

PRO TIP The Minnesota Historical Society provides a range of tours featuring history that makes the Twin Cities unique, including the F. Scott Fitzgerald Walking Tour. Tickets can be purchased at mnhs.org. Another great resource is fitzgeraldinsaintpaul.org.

CORNER LOT DIVER

Why is there a deep-sea diver standing on a west suburban street corner?

A life-size, commercial diver is about the last thing you'd expect to see while passing by the corner of Vicksburg Lane and Ninth Avenue North in Plymouth—a lovely Minneapolis suburb, but one that is nowhere near the sea. Carved from a tree trunk, the roadside surprise is illuminated by a light inside the helmet's faceplate. Another light shines upward from the ground.

Jack and Delores Gause moved into the house on that property in 1960 when the street was still dirt and houses were sparse. A tree died on the corner the same year that Jack's brother died. So Jack hired a local woodcarver to transform the tree into a tribute to the local commercial diving business his father started in 1937—C. H. Gause & Sons Commercial Divers.

As a diver, Jack, along with his brother and dad, plunged into rivers and lakes throughout the country laying cables, inspecting power plants, hunting for bodies, and blowing up dams with dynamite. Eventually Jack took over the business, but by the time he reached his forties, he was ready to hang up his gear. It's his own helmet on the corner diver's head. "It's the last remaining diver in our family," Jack said in an interview for *Secret Twin Cities* two months before he passed away in his home on July 6, 2019.

But diving is only part of Jack's legacy. A father of three who was married to Delores for sixty-seven years, he was also a former Navy sailor, math teacher, and wrestling icon. Prior to being inducted into the National Wrestling Hall of

---

The late Jack Gause learned how to dive on the job at the age of fifteen. "My dad put me in a suit and pushed me off the ledge," he said.

The deep-sea diver carving is illuminated at night by a light inside the helmet, the same helmet that the late Jack Gause used while working as a commercial diver for his dad's business.

DEEP-SEA DIVER AND WRESTLING LEGEND

WHAT The story behind a roadside deep-sea diver

WHERE Corner of Vicksburg Lane and Ninth Avenue North, Plymouth

COST Free

PRO TIP Less than a block north of the diver is the Luce Line Trail, a sixty-three-mile former railroad grade developed for hiking, horseback riding, mountain biking, snowmobiling, and skiing. From Plymouth, the limestone surfaced trail runs thirty miles west to Winsted.

Fame in 2015, he founded the wrestling program at St. Cloud State in 1949 while he was a freshman, served as a wrestling coach in Minnesota for thirty years, officiated the Pan-American Games and four World Cups, and refereed seven World Tournaments and the 1976 Olympic Games in Montreal.

MEGA MOVE

Which six-million-pound theater was moved a quarter mile on dollies and why?

Across the street from the giant rainbow-hued Bob Dylan mural is the oldest existing theater building in downtown Minneapolis. And since 1999, it's also carried the Guinness World Record title as the largest structure ever moved on rubber-wheeled dollies.

Today, primarily used as a dance auditorium, it's called the Goodale Theater and is connected to The Cowles Center for Dance & the Performing Arts. But when it was built in 1910, it was a freestanding Broadway venue called the Shubert Theatre. At that time, it was located on Seventh Street in a stretch of downtown known as Block E.

People who've been around the Twin Cities for a while remember that in the 1970s and '80s, Block E—bounded by Hennepin Avenue, Sixth Street, Seventh Street, and First Avenue North—was an epicenter of seedy bars, flophouses, adult movie theaters, and tacky street-front signage. In 1985, the city council voted to demolish it all and start over with a clean slate. Some people were up in arms. Others rejoiced. After a ten-year battle to save the historic Shubert Theatre from the wrecking ball, a proposal submitted by the nonprofit Artspace Projects to move the building around the corner to its current location was accepted.

The oldest existing theater in downtown Minneapolis has been many things since it opened in 1910, from a Broadway venue and burlesque show house to an evangelical church and movie theater. Now it's a dance auditorium and a Guinness World Record holder.

The Shubert Theatre, now known as the Goodale Theater, brought Broadway to Minneapolis in 1910, attracting the likes of Mae West and the Marx Brothers. When it was lifted up and moved around the corner in 1999, it was the heaviest move ever attempted on rubber-wheeled dollies.

One hundred hydraulic jacks were used to lift the massive structure, while seventy dollies formed a foundation for the short—but daunting—journey. Before successfully setting it down at its new spot, the mover needed to move the building a half block, make a ninety-degree turn, go sideways another block, then swing forty-five degrees to the north to avoid hitting other buildings. From start to finish, this mega-move took twelve exceedingly tense days.

GOODALE THEATER, FORMERLY THE SHUBERT THEATRE

WHAT Historic theater and its world-record move around the corner

WHERE 528 Hennepin Ave., Minneapolis (joined with The Cowles Center)

COST Free

PRO TIP Take time to check out the mini-mural in front of the open parking lot next to the theater. It's a series of portraits and stories that artist Stephanie Glaros has since turned into a book called *Humans of Minneapolis.*

A SNAZZIER SNELLING

What do the murals on Snelling Avenue North represent?

For many of us, Snelling Avenue just north of I-94 has simply been the corridor to get to the State Fair while daydreaming about hotdish on a stick. But what many don't know is that this historically drab-looking area, dubbed "Little Africa," is home to richly diverse businesses owned by immigrants and women.

And now, thanks to the Midway Murals Project, that stretch is at least a little more eye-catching.

In 2015, local artists dotted the half-mile stretch with a few stunning murals on buildings. The effort was initiated by Jonathan Oppenheimer, a University of Minnesota student who secured a grant from the Knights Arts Challenge Saint Paul. The murals don't simply help enliven the neighborhood—they also create important conversations. The theme that ties the murals together is "Starting Anew." That could be interpreted in several ways, including the immigrant experience, a brighter future, or the changing face of Saint Paul.

Painted on the Snelling Café at 638 Snelling Avenue is *Convergence* by BLASTER. It features dove feathers and elements of outer space, reflecting a galaxy of cultures. Displayed on the plaza at 555 Snelling Avenue is Lori Greene's Ethiopian-inspired mural, called *Berbere*, created with pieces of broken, colored tile. Gracing the outside of Kim's Oriental (Korean) Market at 689 Snelling Avenue is Yuya Negishi's

MIDWAY MURALS PROJECT

WHAT A series of murals on a half-mile stretch of Snelling Avenue North

WHERE Hamline Midway neighborhood (a few blocks from Allianz Field)

COST Free

PRO TIP Midway Used and Rare Books, a literary treasure in the Twin Cities for well over fifty years, is one block from the *Braided* mural.

The mural Braided *features the owner of the nearby Sunshine Beauty Salon, her daughter, and a coworker in a vibrant swirl of cultural patterns. The mural was designed to highlight the role of females in the immigrant story and the importance of maintaining one's individuality while interweaving into a community to make it stronger. See it in full color in the center insert.*

Japanese-inspired mural *Birth of a New Day*, which features a phoenix and the glorious sun.

Perhaps the most eye-catching of the group is Greta McLain's mural *Braided*, which wraps around the plaza at 512 Snelling Avenue. It features Freweini Sium, the owner of the nearby Sunshine Beauty Salon, smiling as her hair is braided by her coworker into a swirl of African, Norwegian, Mexican, Hmong, and Native American patterns. The beautiful young girl featured on the far right end of the mural is Sium's daughter.

With the common theme of "starting anew," the Midway Murals were created not only to enliven Snelling Avenue North but also to bring people into more conversation and connection with one another.

RETRO REPOSITORY

Where can you immerse yourself in the golden age of broadcasting while your kid learns how to dial a rotary phone?

As you weave your way through a nondescript industrial area looking for the Pavek Museum in suburban St. Louis Park, you might wonder if you got the address wrong. But then you turn a corner, and colorful banners hanging from a plain brick building mark the spot. It doesn't look like much on the outside. But inside it's a twelve-thousand-square-foot vintage treasure chest featuring the most spectacular collection of electronic communication equipment anywhere.

Starting off in the lobby, you're greeted by one of the first four-tube color made-for-TV cameras. Off to the right is a 1934 Wurlitzer jukebox that you can play for a nickel. Then enter the exhibit hall and be prepared to be flabbergasted by thousands of radios, microphones, telephones, neon signs, German AEG Magnetophon tape recorders, a 1912 telegraph machine like the one used on the Titanic, and on and on.

There are interactive areas where visitors can put on a news broadcast, participate in old-time radio quiz programs, and learn (or relearn) how to dial a rotary phone. In 2001, a Hall of Fame was added to salute and preserve the careers of on-air personalities and other broadcasting legends from all over Minnesota.

The museum opened in 1988, but the collection started sometime in the 1940s. While Joe Pavek was working as an electronics instructor for the Minneapolis Dunwoody

Take a walk down memory lane while your kids experience what radios, TVs, and phones used to be like.

PAVEK MUSEUM OF BROADCASTING

WHAT History and science of electronic communication

WHERE 3517 Raleigh Ave. S., St. Louis Park

COST Adults and seniors, $8; students, $6

PRO TIP The museum offers several educational programs, including a podcast camp for children and a vintage radio repair class for adults.

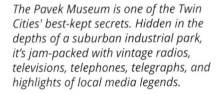

The Pavek Museum is one of the Twin Cities' best-kept secrets. Hidden in the depths of a suburban industrial park, it's jam-packed with vintage radios, televisions, telephones, telegraphs, and highlights of local media legends.

Institute, he became concerned about the radios being torn apart as students learned their trade. So he began sneaking the radios home. From that point on, he never stopped collecting. Eventually, his collection became so immense that the Minnesota Broadcasters Association and Earl Bakken, (inventor of the pacemaker—see "Spark of Life," page 56) stepped in and helped turn it into a nonprofit museum.

WINGED AMBASSADORS

Where do injured raptors inspire humans to better appreciate the natural world?

There are about 482 species of raptors in this world. Whether it's an eagle, hawk, owl, or falcon, they all have three things in common: exceptional eyesight, sharp talons, and a hooked beak. But each of the nearly one thousand sick and injured birds brought to the Raptor Center at the University of Minnesota Saint Paul Campus each year has a story that is unique (and heartbreaking).

Although the goal is to treat, rehabilitate, and release the birds back into the wild, some are deemed unreleasable. A number of the unreleasable stay at the Raptor Center and serve as education ambassadors for their species. Maxime, Luta, and Talon are three of those ambassadors. Maxime, a bald eagle, was discovered alongside a highway with lead poisoning and a dislocated left humerus-ulna joint. Luta, a red-tailed hawk, was noticed in a homeowner's backyard, thin and dehydrated. Talon, a peregrine falcon, was found with the tips of her talons broken off and feathers melted, perhaps from a smokestack or methane burner.

The Raptor Center, a nonprofit functioning within the U of M College of Veterinary Medicine, was founded in the early 1970s by Dr. Gary Duke and Dr. Patrick Redig. Duke was a professor of avian physiology at the university, while Redig was a first-year veterinary student. A Good Samaritan brought four baby great horned owls in need of care to Duke. Redig asked Duke if he could help.

The Raptor Center's clinic includes a surgical suite, indoor flight areas, and other features that allow it to treat over one thousand birds each year.

Maxime, the bald eagle, was discovered alongside a highway with lead poisoning and a dislocated left humerus-ulna joint, possibly due to a collision injury with a power line. Samantha, the great horned owl, was found on a roadside, too, with multiple wing injuries. It's thought that she may have been hit by a vehicle.

Their animal holding area filled up with more and more birds. Eventually, the two birders built a team of staff, volunteers, and interns thanks to grants and donations. The Raptor Center is now a place where students from all over the world come to study and gain hands-on experience.

THE RAPTOR CENTER

WHAT Wildlife hospital and research center specializing in eagles, hawks, owls, and falcons

WHERE University of Minnesota–Saint Paul Campus, 1920 Fitch Ave., Saint Paul

COST $3-$5 with tours every thirty minutes

PRO TIP Displayed at the center and posted on its website are all kinds of ways you, too, can help protect raptors.

BUS STOP BOUQUET

What's the story behind the bus stop with giant steel flowers sprouting out of it?

Nothing says "Welcome to Minneapolis" more than the *Spoonbridge and Cherry* sculpture at the Walker Art Center Sculpture Garden. And nothing says "Welcome to *North* Minneapolis" quite like the lovely bus stop at the corner of Penn and Broadway avenues.

City of Minneapolis Art in Public Places wanted to create a focal point on that bustling corner that would serve as a cheerful landmark in a neighborhood that sometimes gets a bad rap. So it commissioned Marjorie Pitz, a landscape architect and public artist, to create a bus shelter that resembles a giant vase with large, vibrant steel flowers sprouting through its roof. It has a rather remarkable story.

When the sculpture was about 95 percent complete in the spring of 2011, a deadly tornado packing 125 mph winds plowed across North Minneapolis, causing two deaths, dozens of injuries, and mass property damage. The artsy bus shelter was at the epicenter of the storm. Pitz was out of town at the time. When she saw reports of the tornado on the news, she was worried the massive, heavy flowers might've flown off and hurt people. But like a beacon of strength amongst the toppled-over trees, power lines, stoplights, and buildings all around it, the structure remained intact with only minor damage. The

---

After surviving a tornado that ripped through the area in 2011, the *Blossoms of Hope* transit shelter in North Minneapolis—made of aluminum, steel, and glass and disguised as a vibrant vase of towering blooms—serves as a bright and welcoming landmark.

Blossoms of Hope was created by landscape architect and public artist Marjorie Pitz and commissioned by City of Minneapolis Art in Public Places.

BLOSSOMS OF HOPE BUS SHELTER

WHAT North Minneapolis bus shelter that looks like a giant bouquet

WHERE Corner of Penn and Broadway avenues, Minneapolis

COST Free

PRO TIP Buy a cookie (or a dozen) at the nearby Cookie Cart (see "Heavenly Cookies," page 60).

flowers had been designed to bend and sway in the wind.

In the days following the tornado, a building next to the bus stop was used as an emergency shelter with food, water, and clothing for those who had lost their homes. It was the place where people helped other people find a way to go on with their lives. And it was that spirit of generosity and humanity in the storm's aftermath that inspired the shelter to be named *Blossoms of Hope*.

SOURCES

1. **Wonderland Off I-35**
    Personal visit to Hot Sam's, April 23, 2019; www.minnesota.cbslocal.com/2014/08/10/
    finding-minnesota-the-shark-the-rocket-other-odditiesalong-i-35; www.youtube.com/
    watch?v=LR0ppXNvTXs; www.minnesota.cbslocal.com/2014/08/10/finding-minnesota-the-
    shark-the-rocket-other-oddities-along-i-35.

2. *Sidewalk Harp*
    www.codaworx.com/project/sidewalk-harp; www.jenlewinstudio.com/sidewalk-harp;
    www.startribune.com/international-artist-to-install-three-story-public-art-atminneapolis-st-p;
    www.bethematch.org/about-us/our-story; www.mspmag.com/arts-and-culture/perfect-
    strangers; www.airportfoundation.org/programsservices/arts-culture/commissioned-artwork/
    mosaics; www.startribune.com/international-artist-to-install-three-story-public-art-at-
    minneapolis-st-paul-airport-sterminal-1/481111081; www.airportfoundation.org/programs-
    services/arts-culture/commissioned-artwork/restrooms. Email correspondence with Lauren
    Miller, May 10, 2019; (And, I've personally played it a few times.)

3. **James J. Hill Stairs of Pain**
    Personal climb up and down, May 28, 2019; Millett, Larry. 2007. *AIA Guide to the Twin Cities: The
    Essential Source on the Architecture of Minneapolis and Saint Paul*; Minnesota Historical Society;
    www.saintpaulhistorical.com/items/show/314;
    www.minnpost.com/stroll; www.planning.org/greatplaces/streets/2008/summitavenue.htm;
    www.tpt.org/james-j-hill-empire-builder; www.midwestweekends.com/plan_a_trip/history_
    heritage/historic_houses/summit_avenue_st_paul.html; www.biography.com/people/james-j-
    hill-38025; www.mnhs.org/hillhouse/learn/james-j-hill.

4. **Underground Library**
    Email correspondence with Kris Kiesling, Elmer L. Andersen Director of Archives and Special
    Collections, May 13, 2019; www.lib.umn.edu/andersen/about-building; www.soudan.umn.edu/
    outreach/mural.shtml; www.johnweeks.com/tour/odd/odd_downtown.html; www.continuum.
    umn.edu/2018/10/elmer-l-andersen-library-2-0; www.minnpost.com/stroll/2015/10/
    subterranean-caverns-protect-us-andersenlibrary-collections.

5. **Sister Gift Exchange**
    Personal visit to Phalen Regional Park, August 15, 2019; Email correspondences with
    representative from the Minnesota China Friendship Garden Society, April 24, 2019;
    www.twincities.com/2017/07/20/st-paul-chinese-garden-to-featurepavilion-donated-by-sister-
    city-changsha; www.woodburybulletin.com/news/traffic-and-construction/4522169-st-paul-
    changsha-china-friendship-gardenhost-open-house%3famp; www.hastingsstargazette.com/
    news/traffic-andconstruction/4522169-st-paul-changsha-china-friendship-garden-host-open-
    house; www.stpaul.gov/departments/parks-recreation/design-construction/currentprojects/
    phalen-regional-park-chinese.

6. **Lost and Found**
    Personal visit with store owner Amy Buchanan, May 15, 2019; www.atlasobscura.com/places/
    center-for-lost-objects; www.leversonbudke.com/center-for-lost-objectsst-paul.

7. **In the Shadows**
    Many walks along Nicollet Mall; Email correspondences with assistants to Seitu Jones and
    Ta-coumba Aiken, May 29, 2019; www.startribune.com/a-close-look-atminneapolis-remade-
    nicollet-mall/457455523; www.nicolletmallart.org/restoringshadows-of-spirit;
    www.nicolletmallart.org/shadows-of-spirit-whats-invisiblebecomes-visible.

8. **Reverence for Rock**
    Visits to some of the sculptures in spring 2019; www.mprnews.org/story/2006/05/23/
    minnesotarocks; www.thecurrent.org/feature/2006/06/30/minnesotarocksrevisited;
    www.publicartstpaul.org.

9. **The Hollow**
    Personal visit to Swede Hollow, May 10, 2019; Discussion with Steve Trimble, longtime local

resident and member of editorial board for the Ramsey County Historical Society, August 30, 2019; www.mnopedia.org/place/swede-hollow; www.saintpaulhistorical.com/items/show/294; www.saintpaulalmanac.org/saint-paul-stories/history/meridel-lesueur-recallsswede-hollow-before-prohibition; www.twincities.com/1999/05/12/swede-hollowsheltered-immigrants-as-they-began-pursuit-of-american-dream; www.newmusicmn.org/swede-hollow-opera-ann-millikan; www.lowerphalencreek.org/swedehollow; www.minnpost.com/stroll/2013/05/exploring-swede-hollow-once-neighborhoodcarved-out-wild; www.knightfoundation.org/articles/swede-hollow-is-the-subject-ofa-new-opera-and-the-site-of-its-premiere.

10. **Temptress of Teas**
Interview and personal tour of Bingley's with Julia Matson, May 15, 2019; www.daynab.com/blog/2018/6/11/its-about-tea-time; www.southwestjournal.com/news/biz-buzz/2015/02/coming-soon-bingleys-teas-tasting-room; www.twincitiesgeek.com/2017/01/bingleys-is-the-twin-cities-best-kept-secret-for-tea-lovers; www.bingleysteas.com.

11. **Landmark Legends and Letters**
Self-guided tours, January 15 and July 21, 2019; Phone conversation with Kate Cooper, Schubert Museum director, September 17, 2019; Email correspondence with Amy Mino, executive director, Minnesota Landmarks, April 17, 2019; Huber, Molly. "Schubert Club." *MNopedia*, Minnesota Historical Society. http://www.mnopedia.org/group/schubert-club; www.exploreminnesota.com/things-to-do/2808/the-schubertclub-museum; www.landmarkcenter.org/about/history.htm.

12. **Where's *Scherzo*?**
Lost Twin Cities III—Twin Cities PBS; Visit to Calhoun Towers and tour of Foshay Tower Museum, April 30, 2019; Phone interview with Brian Short, May 8, 2019; Phone conversation with Calhoun Towers developer Robb Bader, May 7, 2019; Aamodt, Britt. "Foshay Tower." *MNopedia*, Minnesota Historical Society, www.mnopedia.org/structure/foshay-tower; www.southwestjournal.com/news/development/2018/02/calhoun-towers-developerdreams-big; www.finance-commerce.com/2016/12/bader-buys-calhoun-towersin-minneapolis; www.finance-commerce.com/2019/01/bader-buy-connectscalhoun-towers-to-transit-affordability; www.minneapolisnorthwest.com/blog/blog-atop-the-foshaytower-observation-deck; www.nytimes.com/1982/11/22/obituaries/robert-e-shortbusinessman-dies.html.

13. **Neon-Lit Island**
Email correspondence with Chris Steller, longtime resident of Nicollet Island, August 21, 2019; Several personal visits to the island; Hage, Christopher, and Rushika Hage. 2010. Nicollet Island: History and Architecture. Nodin Press; www.m.startribune.com/how-did-nicollet-island-become-parkland-with-privatehousing-on-it/508757581/?om_rid=2624682441&om_mid=298672585; www.homesmsp.com/2016/05/nicollet-island-the-only-inhabited-island-on-the-mississippi.html; www.minneapolisparks.org/parks__destinations/parks__lakes/boom_island_park; www.preserveminneapolis.org/events/nicollet-island-walking-tour-47e3n; www.fmr.org/nicollet-island; www.fasthorseinc.com/blog/2017/07/nicolletisland.

14. **Grown-Up Dioramas**
Email correspondence with Tim Quady, April 12–14, 2019; www.twincities.com/2018/07/12/the-bell-museums-dioramas-zeroing-in-on-minnesotas-biomesartfully; www.rhinocentral.com; www.finance-commerce.com/2018/06/engineering-feat-brings-old-new-exhibits-tobell-museums-new-home; www.startribune.com/the-bell-is-back-and-better-thanever/487945561; www.bellmuseum.umn.edu; www.iida-northland.org/events/bellmuseum-forum; www.aia-mn.org/bell-museum; www.twincities.com/2015/01/03/eagans-blue-rhino-studio-brings-mammoths-to-the-masses; www.fox9.com/news/eagan-artists-bring-dinosaurs-back-to-life.

15. **Bills and Bowling Balls**
Phone interview with Ted Casper, August 8, 2019; Personal visit to The Nook, April 16, 2019; www.twincities.com/2010/07/06/the-nook-is-taking-over-ran-ham-bowlingcenter; www.minnpost.com/stroll/2013/09/street-signs-framed-jerseys-hamlinerandolph-area-one-annotated-neighborhood; www.citypages.com/best-of/2014/sports-and-recreation/ran-ham-bowling-center-7365678; www.leversonbudke.com/nook-basement-st-paul.

16. **Feel the Beat**
Sat in on a class at the Drum Center, August 20, 2019; Email correspondences with Drum Center staff, April 9–14, 2019; www.monitorsaintpaul.com/womens-drumcenter-beating-the-drums-in-their-new-space; www.womensdrumcenter.org/aboutus; www.givemn.org/organization/Womens-Drum-Center; www.facebook.com/womensdrumcenter.

17. **Tangled Tower**
Personal visits to the tower January 16, 2019, and August 15, 2019; www.forgottenminnesota.com/2012/02/the-guardians-of-health; www.m.startribune.com/minnesota-landmark-washburn-water-tower-was-a-soaring-designachievement/475596193; www.atlasobscura.com/places/washburn-park-watertower; www.minnpost.com/stroll/2012/09/tangletown-neighborhood-feels-its-name; www.minneapolismn.gov/hpc/landmarks/hpc_landmarks_prospect_ave_401_washburn_park_water_tower; www.collections.mnhs.org/MNHistoryMagazine/articles/49/v49i01p019-028.pdf.

18. **East Meets West**
Phone interview with Jerry Allan, April 10, 2019; Visit to the Peace Garden, May 26, 2019; www.history.com/topics/world-war-ii/bombing-of-hiroshimaand-nagasaki; www.southwestjournal.com/news/2015/08/peace-gardenceremony-commemorates-nuclear-attack; www.vimeo.com/135733738; www.minneapolisparks.org/parks__destinations/gardens__bird_sanctuaries/lyndale_park_peace_garden; www.democracyconvention.org/conference/session/hiroshima-nagasaki-commemoration-peace-garden-lake-harriet; www.twincities.com/2015/08/14/st-paul-nagasaki-celebrating-60-years-as-sister-cities; www.atomicheritage.org/history/bombings-hiroshima-and-nagasaki-1945; www.homesmsp.com/2011/05/flowers-are-blooming-at-lyndale-park.html.

19. **Our Prince**
Email correspondence with local music historian Kristen Zschomler, August 27–31, 2019; Zschomler, Kristen. "Prince (1958–2016)." *MNopedia*, Minnesota Historical Society. www.mnopedia.org/person/prince-1958-2016; Delegard, Kirsten, and Michael J. Lansing. "Prince and the Making of the Minneapolis Mystique." Middle West Review 5, no. 1 (2018): 1–24; www://muse.jhu.edu/article/705736; www.digitours.augsburg.edu/tours/show/3; www.ew.com/article/2016/04/21/prince-deadminneapolis-mayor-betsy-hodges-tribute; www.startribune.com/the-life-of-princeas-told-by-the-people-who-knew-him/376586581; www.citypages.com/music/apresent-to-minneapolis-amazing-prince-mural-emerges-in-uptown-8229678.

20. **Assassinated Photo**
Personal visit and conversation with bartender at Black Forest Inn, January 3, 2019; Email correspondence with Erica Christ, August 6, 2019; www.startribune.com/black-forest-inn-celebrates-50-years-with-a-weekend-festival/303452521; www.mspmag.com/arts-and-culture/amazing-lore-legends-and-myths; www.blackforestinnmpls.com/pgs/art.ph.

21. **World's Quietest Place**
Phone interview with Steve Orfield, March 9, 2019; www.bbc.com/future/story/20170526-inside-the-quietest-place-on-earth; www.startribune.com/quietest-place-on-earth-finds-purpose-in-healing-humans/450258993; www.today.com/health/therapeutic-silence-one-quietest-rooms-world-t130981; www.atlasobscura.com/places/orfield-labs-quiet-chamber; www.orfieldlabs.com/pdfarticles.html; www.youtube.com/watch?v=9mPbL5ewK7Q&feature=share; www.sound80.com/about-us; www.minnesota.cbslocal.com/2016/06/26/finding-minnesota-orfield-laboratories.

22. **Winter Carnival Trove**
Personal visit to West Saint Paul Antiques, May 15, 2019; www.wintercarnival.com; www.weststpaulantiques.com/wintercarnival.html; www.vulcans.org/content/legend.

23. **The Perfect Gem**
Email correspondence with Robert Greenberg of The 614 Company, August 21, 2019; Self-guided tours of the Young-Quinlan building, April 30 and July 25, 2019; Kronick, Richard L., and Lisa Middag. "Young-Quinlan Building," Minneapolis Historical, www.minneapolishistorical.org/

items/show/170; www.minnpost.com/stroll/2015/02/magic-and-elegance-elevators-downtown-minneapolis; www.m.startribune.com/minnesota-s-last-elevator-operators/257249671; www.kare11.com/video/life/new-young-quinlan-building-exhibit/89-2421895; www.forgottenminnesota.com/2014/03/the-queen-of-minneapolis; www.youtube.com/watch?v=fcJiiXOoOPE.

24. **Longfellow Zoo Artifacts**
Personal visits to Longfellow Gardens, July 19, 2019, and August 15, 2019; www.minnesotaschoolofbotanicalart.com/styled; www.collections.mnhs.org/MNHistoryMagazine/articles/55/v55i08p364-373.pdf; www.growlermag.com/the-inimitable-robert-fish-jones-the-dandy-zookeeper-of-minneapolis; www.southwestjournal.com/voices/historyapolis/2014/05/the-demise-of-the-longfellow-zoological-gardens; www.southwestjournal.com/voices/historyapolis/2014/05/downtown-minneapolis-once-home-to-eccentric-zoo; www.bigboytravel.com/minnesota/minneapolis/minnehaha-falls-walking-tour; www.minneapolisparks.org/parks__destinations/gardens__bird_sanctuaries/longfellow_gardens.

25. **Above the Rest**
Self-guided tour, January 17, 2019; Nelson, Paul. "St. Paul City Hall and Ramsey County Courthouse." *MNopedia*, Minnesota Historical Society. http://www.mnopedia.org/structure/st-paul-city-hall-and-ramsey-county-courthouse; Ramsey County Courthouse self-guided tour brochure; Millett, Larry. 2007. *AIA Guide to the Twin Cities: The Essential Source on the Architecture of Minneapolis and Saint Paul*. Minnesota Historical Society; www.spytwincities.com/tc-ogling-vision-of-peace-st-paul-city-hall-1086.

26. **Slice of Mexico**
Visit to Mercado Central, July 19, 2019; www.southsidepride.com/2018/04/16/mercado-central-great-place-for-latino-businesses-to-grow; www.heavytable.com/east-lake-checklist-mercado-central; www.mimercadocentral.com.

27. **Capitol's Uncovered Mottoes**
Self-guided tour, July 28, 2019; Email correspondence with Brian Pease, Minnesota State Capitol Historic Site Manager, April 22, 2019; www.mnhs.org/preserve/rathskeller.php; www.cassgilbertsociety.org/architect/bio.html; www.m.startribune.com/minnesota-state-capitol-restaurant-serves-a-cheeseburger-worthy-of-thebuilding-s-splendor/477004873; www.minnesotamonthly.com/Blogs/Taste-Blog/The-Best-8-Burger-in-The-Twin-Cities; www.minnesota.cbslocal.com/2014/12/12/secret-doors-hidden-skylights-inside-the-capitols-restoration; www.johnweeks.com/tour/cassgilbert/index.html.

28. **Spark of Life**
Self-guided tour of Bakken Museum, November 7, 2018; www.mspmag.com/artsand-culture/amazing-lore-legends-and-myths; www.offthebeatenpagetravel.com/tag/bakken-museum; www.telegraph.co.uk/obituaries/2018/10/30/earl-bakken-engineer-whosechildhood-fascination-frankenstein; www.earlbakken.com/content/timeline/timeline.html; www.onlinelibrary.wiley.com/doi/pdf/10.1002/clc.4960240515; Email correspondence with Laura Whittet, November 19, 2019.

29. **Where the Waters Meet**
Personal hike out to Bdote, September 18, 2019; Email correspondence with Eden Bart from the Minnesota Humanities Center, July 9, 2019; Westerman, Gwen, and Bruce White. 2012. *Mni Sota Makoce: The Land of the Dakota*. Minnesota Historical Society; www.usdakotawar.org; www.bdotememorymap.org/memory-map/#; www.usdakotawar.org/history/dakotahomeland-land-lifestyle/bdote; www.startribune.com/4-dakota-landmarks-hide-inplain-sight-along-the-mississippi-river/491059421; www.mnhum.org/native-nationsminnesota/why-treaties-matter; www.mnhs.org/fortsnelling/learn/us-dakota-war.

30. **Heavenly Cookies**
Personal visit to the shop, May 13, 2019; www.cookiecart.org; www.m.startribune.com/obituaries/detail/140287; www.mprnews.org/story/2018/05/17/bakery-thatteaches-kids-life-lessons-expands-st-paul.

31. **Z Puppets!**
Email correspondences with Shari Aronson, March 21–24, 2019; www.minnesotamonthly.com/arts-entertainment/z-puppets-celebrates-20-years; www.zpuppets.org.

32. **Largest Lite-Brite**
Self-guided tour of Union Depot, December 8, 2018; www.ta-coumba.com; www.lowertown.info/news/domination-corporation-at-northern-spark-2017; www.startribune.com/new-restaurant-at-union-depot-gives-st-paul-passengers-more-mealchoices/491833221; www.tcdailyplanet.net/behind-st-pauls-lite-brite-challenge; www.google.com/amp/s/www.twincities.com/2016/03/18/st-paul-union-depot-26-things-to-know-for-its-90th-anniversary/amp.

33. **Wild Thing**
Email correspondence with Collette Morgan, May 22, 2019; Personal visits to the store over the years; www.writersblock.loft.org/2014/10/10/3535/lit_chat_meet_collette_morgan; www.southwestjournal.com/features/2016/05/wild-rumpus-books-named-best-in-u-s; www.growlermag.com/mill-wild-rumpusnamed-best-childrens-bookstore-in-u-s; www.authorpublishingservices.com/wildrumpus-because-were-all-a-little-wild-at-heart.

34. **Mr. Jimmy's Bench**
Interview with Bob Bolles, Mr. Jimmy's good friend, January 9, 2019; www.swnewsmedia.com/lakeshore_weekly/news/excelsior-s-roving-ambassador-diesmr-jimmy/article_7f9ab161-7244-5ab9-8460-550fbdb497ac.html; www.minnpost.com/arts-culture/2015/06/stones-lore-jagger-and-mr-jimmy-excelsior; www.swnewsmedia.com/lakeshore_weekly/news/local/he-belonged-to-excelsior-jamesmr-jimmy-hutmaker-was-more/article_1816d0d8-fc2e-5320-bf33-7124d9f9965d.html.

35. **Livestock Universe**
Visit to the stockyard landmarks, January 3, 2019; "Conversations of History in South Saint Paul" Facebook group; www.twincities.com/2009/06/20/armour-a-way-of-life; www.dakotahistory.org/images/history/South-St.-Paul-Voice-History-Archive-by-Lois-Glewwe.pdf; www.startribune.com/south-st-paul-from-cow-town-to-riverfront-attraction/140983383; www2.mnhs.org/library/findaids/00485.xml; www.mississippivalleytraveler.com/south-st-paul; www.postbulletin.com/more-memories-from-the-south-st-paul-stockyards/article_59152bf6-04d6-591c-8d12-2666f7339782.html.

36. **Falls Fiasco**
Self-guided tour of Heritage Trail and Water Power Park, May 6, 2019; Huber, Molly. "St. Anthony Falls Tunnel Collapse, October 5, 1869." *MNopedia*, Minnesota Historical Society. www.mnopedia.org/event/st-anthony-falls-tunnel-collapse-october-5-1869; www.historyapolis.com/blog/2016/02/22/minneapolis-is-ruined-the-tunnel-disaster-of-1869; www.esci.umn.edu/courses/1001/1001_kirkby/SAFL/WEBSITEPAGES/5.html; www.nps.gov/miss/planyourvisit/stanfall.htm; www.city-data.com/us-cities/The-Midwest/Minneapolis-History.html#ixzz5XuDolH8I.

37. **White Castle #8**
Email correspondence with co-owner of Xcentric Goods, June 20, 2019; Personal visit to the store, July 2019; www.m.startribune.com/what-s-the-story-behind-the-marooned-minneapolis-white-castle/508773862; www.mentalfloss.com/article/64759/21-crave-worthy-facts-about-white-castle; www.thedailymeal.com/eat/9-things-you-didn-t-know-about-white-castle; www.consumerist.com/2015/07/14/the-white-castle-story-the-birth-of-fast-food-the-burger-revolution; www.citypages.com/restaurants/lyndale-white-castle-buildings-mysteries-revealed-6604351; www.xcentricgoods.com; www.southwestjournal.com/news/biz-buzz/2015/03/xcentric-goods-moves-into-white-castle-building-on-lyndale; www.mnhs.org/preserve/nrhp/property_overview.cfm-propertyID=31.html.

38. **Really Big Snowman**
Personal visit to North Saint Paul, December 15, 2018.; www.northstpaul.org/299/Worlds-Largest-Snowman; www.startribune.com/day-trip-north-st-paul-is-an-old-style-small-town-in-town/267707681; www.startribune.com/north-st-paul-s-44-foot-20-ton-snowman-is-showing-its-age/257599551.

39. **"Super-Secret" Speakeasy**
Stopped in at Volstead's for dinner and cocktails, August 31, 2019; www.mnopedia.org/thing/national-prohibition-act-volstead-act; www.startribune.com/dreamcatchers-can-welcome-new-neighborhood-speakeasy-to-uptown/366586141; www.minnesota.cbslocal.com/2018/04/05/best-speakeasy-minneapolis; www.mspmag.com/eat-and-drink/the-secret-speakeasy-in-uptown.

40. **Nomadic Treasures**
Personal tour of museum, May 11, 2019; www.citypages.com/calendar/somalis-minnesota/463684983; www.mnhs.org/historycenter/activities/museum/somalis; www.minnpost.com/politics-policy/2017/08/complicated-reality-behind-story-somali-communitys-success-minnesota; www.minnesota.cbslocal.com/2011/01/19/good-question-why-did-somalis-locate-here; www.mprnews.org/story/2013/10/18/arts/somali-artifact-cultural-museum.

41. **Traces of Trolleys**
Email correspondence with representative of Minnesota Streetcar Museum, August 12, 2019; Personal visit to the sealed-up Selby Tunnel, May 20, 2019; Nelson, Paul. "The Streetcar Era." Saint Paul Historical, www.saintpaulhistorical.com/items/show/151; www.youtube.com/watch?v=sbbe_nRBrOE; www.minnpost.com/mnopedia/2016/03/thirty-years-electric-streetcars-ruled-twin-cities-streets; www.minnpost.com/community-voices/2014/02/streetcars-belong-safely-tucked-our-most-cherished-memories; www.johnweeks.

42. **Playground Museum**
Email correspondences with Colleen Sheehy, president and executive director, Public Art Saint Paul, December 7, 2018 and June 19, 2019; Personal visit to the park, January 15, 2019; www.publicartstpaul.org/project/western-sculpture-park/#about_the_project; www.minnesota.cbslocal.com/2012/01/09/exploring-westernsculpture-park-in-st-paul; www.streets.mn/2017/09/27/it-looks-like-the-suburbs; www.businesswire.com/news/home/20170616005330/en/Ecolab-Donating-Iconic-Sculpture-Public-Art-Saint.

43. **BLIND Is Beauty**
Guided tour of BLIND, Inc., with Dick Davis, building historian, August 12, 2019; www.blindinc.org; www.nfb.org; www.startribune.com/preparing-his-granddaughterfor-a-life-without-sight/431205983; www.members.tcq.net/nfbmn/bulletins/su17.htm#_Toc491022617

44. **Limb Makers**
Personal tour of Winkley's with Alex Gruman CO, CTO, Winkley Orthotics & Prosthetics, April 2019; Cartwright, R. L. "Artificial Limb Industry in Minneapolis." *MNopedia*, Minnesota Historical Society. www.mnopedia.org/artificial-limbindustry-minneapolis; www.winkley.com; www.hometownsource.com/sun_post/golden-valley-company-marks-years-in-prosthetics/article_35032e91-5317-54d6-8197-ff6397caccb7.html; www.growlermag.com/next-gen-limb-design; www.startribune.newspapers.com/clip/13753979/star_tribune; www.collections.mnhs.org/MNHistoryMagazine/articles/57/v57i02p086-097.pdf; www.esci.umn.edu/courses/1001/1001_kirkby/SAFL/WEBSITEPAGES/4.html; www.minnpost.com/mnopedia/2014/07/minnesotas-first-medical-device-industry-artificial-limbs.

45. **Old Dives and Pig's Eye**
Visit to The Spot, May 15, 2019; www.startribune.com/the-chapel-175-years-agothat-led-to-st-paul/390808161; www.visitsaintpaul.com/blog/best-saint-paul-divebars; www.minnesotamonthly.com/Food-Drink/What-Makes-a-Minnesota-Bar-a-Dive; www.citypages.com/restaurants/the-drinkers-guide-to-authentic-st-paul-dive-barsby-neighborhood/433901623; www.web.archive.org/web/20080329143104; www.lareau.org/pep-p.html; www.growlermag.com/the-not-so-complete-history-ofpierre-pigs-eye-parrant.

46. **Club Med for Swans**
Phone conversation and email correspondences with Jim Lawrence, August 17–28, 2019; Email correspondence with Margaret Smith, executive director of The Trumpeter Swan Society, July 20, 2019; www.atlasobscura.com/places/swan-park; www.ci.monticello.mn.us/swanpark; www.exploreminnesota.com/things-todo/4309/swan-park-mississippi-drive;

www.midwestweekends.com/plan_a_trip/nature/birds_wildlife/swans_monticello_minnesota.
html.

47. **The Smiling Building**
Visit to the building and park, April 19, 2019; www.minneapolishistorical.org/items/show/166;
www.blochcancer.org/about/cancer-survivors-parks; www.johnweeks.com/tour/odd/odd_
downtown.html; www.finance-commerce.com/2012/11/buildingblocks-marquette-plaza;
www.emporis.com/buildings/122713/marquette-plazaminneapolis-mn-usa; www.minnpost.
com/cityscape/2012/09/cancer-survivors-parkmaking-space-place.

48. **Remembering Rondo**
Personal visit to the plaza, April 17, 2019; Alam, Ehsan. "Rondo Neighborhood, St. Paul."
MNopedia, Minnesota Historical Society. www.mnopedia.org/place/rondoneighborhood-st-
paul; www.libguides.mnhs.org/rondo; www.rondoavenueinc.org/who-we-are3;
www.rememberingrondo.org; www.twincities.com/2016/06/10/st-paul-rondo-neighborhood-
interstate-94-bridges-ttribute; www.macalester.edu. news/2016/03/history-harvest/#/0;
www.rondoavenueinc.org/reconciliation; www.aia-mn.org/rondo-commemorative-plaza;
www.libguides.mnhs.org/rondo.

49. **Frank's Fish Fascination**
Self-guided tour of Weisman Art Museum, July 17, 2019; Email correspondence with Diane
Mullin, August 7, 2019; www.fox9.com/news/iconic-standing-glass-fish-removed-from-
sculpture-garden-during-renovations; www.mspmag.com/arts-and-culture/in-medias-res;
www.mprnews.org/story/2016/01/21/walker-art-center-sculpture-garden#gallery; www.wam.
umn.edu/2015/12/07/a-fishstory; www.biography.com/people/frank-gehry-9308278.

50. **Bridge to Nowhere**
Personal visit to the pier on August 17, 2019; www.visitigh.com/attraction/rock-island-swing-
bridge; www.swctc.org/watch-programming/35-city-of-newport-videos/980-rock-island-swing-
bridge; www.co.dakota.mn.us/Government/Board/District4/Documents/50CoolestFreePlaces.
pdf; www.johnweeks.com/river_mississippi/pages/b39.html; www.startribune.com/swing-
bridge-trailhead-in-inver-grove-heights-a-starting-point-for-park-and-trail-users/307636711.

51. **Saintly Fun**
Email correspondence with Sean Aronson, vice president, director, media relations, June
19, 2019; www.saintsbaseball.com; www.nytimes.com/2003/07/17/sports/baseball-minor-
league-notebook-the-saints-keep-them-laughing-in-st-paul.html; www.espn.com/mlb/story/_/
id/14046201/mike-veeck-funniest-man-baseball-making-ballpark-magic-bill-murray;
www.twincities.com/2018/08/15/st-paul-saints-food-fight-video-baseball-game;
www.ballparkdigest.com/2015/05/21/chs-field-st-paul-saints; www.saintsbaseball.com/about/
ownership.

52. **The City's Attic**
Personal tour inside clock tower with Robert McCune, March 13, 2019;
www.municipalbuildingcommission.org/visitors/history; www.mprnews.org/story/2015/08/21/
minneapolis-digital-archive; www.streets.mn/2014/04/07/lost-neighborhoods-and-
forgotten-archives; www.m.startribune.com/a-jumble-of-minneapolis-history-is-
warehoused-in-the-clock-tower-of-city-hall/410441415; www.mcad.edu/features/
field-trip-clock-tower-municipal-archives; www.fox9.com/news/downtown-celebration-
marks-completion-of-city-hall-clock-tower-renovation; www.journalmpls.com/news/2005/09/
city-halls-stories; www.m.startribune.com/historic-minneapolis-city-hall-clock-will-light-up-
again-monday/420253823; www.kare11.com/article/news/local/city-of-mpls-launches-new-
digital-image-archive/89-105430140; www.classicalmpr.org/story/2018/11/26/bells-above-city-
hall-ring-out-a-minneapolis-musical-tradition.

53. **From the Land of Trapeze**
Personal visit to the Trapeze Center, May 10, 2019; www.minnesotamonthly.com/Blogs/
Journeys-Blog/Come-Fly-With-Me-at-Twin-Cities-Trapeze; www.minnpost.com/two-
cities/2013/04/life-slowly-returns-st-pauls-two-shuttered-breweries; www.instinct.thekiti.
com/2016/05/09/swede-hollow-and-old-breweries-in-st-paul; www.millercoorsblog.com/news/

fast-growing-hamms-beer-looks-to-stay-red-hot-in-2018; www.twincitiestrapeze.com; www.startribune.com/st-paul-trapeze-school-has-students-flying-through-the-air/197703081.

54. **Loring's Last Castle**
Personal walk around neighborhood, March 20, 2019; www.forgottenminnesota.com/blog/2019/1/5/h-alden-smith-mansion-in-minneapolis; www.minneapolismn.gov/www/groups/public/@cped/documents/webcontent/wcmsp-206245.pdf; www.pvnworks.com/wellsfamilycenter; www.twincities.com/2017/04/26/mctc-wants-to-sell-underused-minneapolis-mansion-worth-negative-4-2-million; www.mnhs.org/preserve/nrhp/nomination/76001063.pdf; www.journalmpls.com/news/2007/04/downtowns-haunted-house; www.minneapolismn.gov/www/groups/public/@cped/documents/webcontent/wcmsp-206245.pdf; www.w-noordijkinc.com/alden-smith.

55. **Stories on Wheels**
Email correspondence with Kimberly at Saint Paul Almanac, April 10, 2019; www.saintpaulalmanac.org/news/blog/introducing-the-storymobile; www.storymobile.org; www.twincities.com/2017/11/24/st-paul-almanacs-high-tech-media-hub-foundsafe-on-thanksgiving-day; www.m.startribune.com/saint-paul-almanac-searching-forstolen-storymobile-trailer/459380223.

56. **Old-Time Cinema**
Personal visit to the theater, August 2, 2019; www.heightstheater.com/page/aboutus; www.classicalmpr.org/story/2018/06/25/the-heights-organ--the-grandfatherof-film-music; www.minnpost.com/twin-cities-business/2015/03/how-heightstheater-survives-world-multiplexes; www.minnesota.cbslocal.com/2012/03/05/venue-spotlight-heights-theater; www.mspmag.com/arts-and-culture/generalinterest/such-great-heights.

57. **Carnies' Resting Place**
Visit to Lakewood Cemetery, May 26, 2019; www.lakewoodcemetery.com/History_Chapel.html; www.roadsideamerica.com/tip/12123; www.minnpost.com/stroll/2012/10/walk-through-lakewood-cemetery; www.minnesota.publicradio.org/features/2010/05/28-lakewood-cemetery; www.ci.minneapolis.mn.us/hpc/landmarks/hpc_landmarks_hennepin_ave_3600_lakewood_memorial_chapel; www.startribune.com/lakewood-cemetery-to-lure-the-living-with-new-concertseries/478055803.

58. **Harriet Playground Portrait**
Visit to Harriet Island, May 14, 2019; Visit to the Minnesota Woman Suffrage Memorial, July 28, 2019; Email correspondence with Kate Roberts from the Minnesota Historical Society, July 23, 2019; Wingerd, Mary. "Bishop, Harriet E. (1817–1883)." *MNopedia*, Minnesota Historical Society, www.mnopedia.org/person/bishop-harriet-e-1817-1883; www.twincitiestours.com/captains-blog/mississippiriver; www.editions.lib.umn.edu/openrivers/article/a-tour-of-the-mississippi-rivervisitor-center; www.saintpaulhistorical.com/items/show/126; www.youtube.com/watch?v=eJF985ArVEQ; www.usdakotawar.org/history/harriet-bishop#; www.lisastories.com/2018/08/21/harriet-bishop-a-schoolmarm-in-the-wild-west-saintpaul; www.dakotahistory.org/images/history/South-St.-Paul-Voice-History-Archive-by-Lois-Glewwe.pdf.

59. **Weatherball Tributes**
Visit to the Wells Fargo Museum, April 30, 2019; www.minnesota.cbslocal.com/2013/11/14/new-twist-on-downtown-weather-ball-coming-to-nicollet-mall; www.twincities.com/2013/11/26/wcco-tvs-new-weather-watcher-sign-debuts; www.forgottenminnesota.com/2012/03/170; www.minnesota.cbslocal.com/2013/11/14/new-twist-on-downtown-weather-ball-coming-to-nicollet-mall; www.mnhs.org/historycenter/activities/museum/weather-permitting; www.minnesota.cbslocal.com/2013/11/29/wcco-weather-watcher-lights-up-nicollet-mall; www.minnesota.cbslocal.com/2018/01/26/minnecentric-experience.

60. **Once There Were Frogs**
Visit to the farm, August 17, 2019; Email correspondence with Shelby Rutzick from Frogtown Farm, August 8, 2019; Email correspondence with Patricia Ohmans from Frogtown Green, March 22, 2019; www.tpl.org/blog/frogtown-park-and-farm-opens; www.cityparksalliance.org/why-urban-parks-matter/frontline-parks/parks/426-frogtown-park-a-farm; www.twincities.

com/2018/02/19/frogtown-strives-to-begreenest-st-paul-neighborhood-will-host-sustainability-meeting; www.twincities.com/2013/12/03/in-st-pauls-frogtown-a-park-and-urban-farm-set; www.monitorsaintpaul.com/frogtown-park-and-farm-is-one-of-a-kind; www.m.startribune.com/frogtown-park-and-farm-gives-a-st-paul-neighborhood-much-needed-green-space/331179581.

61. **Secret Language School**
Email correspondence with members of the Japanese American Citizens League, August 26, 2019; Personal visit to Historic Fort Snelling, August 18, 2019; DeCarlo, Peter. "Military Intelligence Service Language School (MISLS)." *MNopedia*, Minnesota Historical Society. www.mnopedia.org/group/military-intelligence-service-language-school-misls; www.mnhs.org; www.nps.gov/miss/learn/historyculture/langschool.htm; www.twincities.com/2015/09/10/japanese-americans-recall-world-war-ii-fort-snelling-military-language-operations; www.mprnews.org/story/2015/05/22/japanese-americans-in-the-military-intelligence-service-during-wwii-exhibit; www.startribune.com/mnhs-broadens-how-it-tells-the-state-s-history/474357683; www.startribune.com/historic-fort-snelling-let-s-tell-all-its-stories-the-military-ones-yes-but-others-too/478346403.

62. **The *Mary Tyler Moore* "Extra"**
www.walkermn.com/obituaries/hazel-frederick/article_fb1c0772-6f36-53a5-b01d-ad88cb860c99.html; www.variety.com/2017/tv/news/mary-tyler-moore-best-interviews-oprah-barbara-walters-1201969742; www.mprnews.org/story/2017/01/25/mary-tyler-moore-in-minneapolis; www.abcnews.go.com/Entertainment/story-iconic-mary-tyler-moore-show-opening/story?id=45052349; www.mentalfloss.com/article/69550/15-awfully-big-facts-about-mary-tyler-moore-show; www.m.startribune.com/20-years-ago-mary-met-twin-cities-woman-who-walked-into-opening-credits/411886665; www.cbsnews.com/news/marys-co-star-dies-at-91; www.articles.latimes.com/1999/dec/01/news/mn-39378.

63. **One, Two, Up She Goes!**
Phone interview with Club President Mike Finegan, October 10, 2018; Got personally bounced by the Bouncing Team on October 20, 2018; www.stpaulbouncingteam.org/carnival.html; www.mprnews.org/story/2011/02/05/winter-carnival-bouncing-team; www.twincities.com/2009/01/17/believe-it-or-not-i-was-a-bouncing-girl.

64. **Sky-Rises for Bees**
Email correspondence with Colleen Satyshur at the University of Minnesota Bee Lab, June 17, 2019; Email correspondence with Colleen Sheehy, president and executive director, Public Art Saint Paul, June 19, 2019; www.district10comopark.org/catch_the_buzz_about_the_pollinator_sky_rise.html; www.mcad.edu/news/mcadians-launch-luxury-pollinator-housing; www.publicartstpaul.org/busy-year-busy-bees; www.wam.umn.edu/2019/02/14/bee-real-bee-everywhere; www.publicartstpaul.org/project/bee-real-bee-everywhere/#about_the_project; www.twincities.com/2017/09/11/bee-sky-rise-will-draw-pollinators-to-como-park-lake-phalen.

65. **Lutefisk Hotline**
Personal tour of Olsen's with Don Sobasky, August 12, 2019; www.tcdailyplanet.net/olsen-fish-company-north-minneapolis-home-worlds-largest-lutefisk-processor; www.startribune.com/minneapolis-lutefisk-plant-adapts-to-new-cultures-new-demands/286847571; www.mprnews.org/story/2012/12/04/lutefisk-pickled-herring-olsen-fish-company-minnesota-sounds-and-voices#gallery; www.mnopedia.org/norwegian-immigration-minnesota; www.npr.org/sections/thesalt/2016/12/15/505389094/whats-a-holiday-without-lutefisk-and-a-little-white-lye.

66. **Sixty-Acre Sculpture**
Personal visit to the park October 30, 2019; www.tcdailyplanet.net/sculpture-parks-twin-cities; www.youtube.com/watch?v=scUSQSg9wGg; www.startribune.com/obituary-sculptor-anthony-caponi-was-educator-mentor-art-park-visionary/332586592; www.caponiartpark.org/visit/guidebook; www.twincities.com/2010/06/05/family-outings-caponi-art-park-and-learning-center-in-eagan; Email correspondence with Cheryl Caponi, November 1, 2019.

67. **The Forty-Fifth Parallel**
Personal visit to the Medicine Lake marker, October 9, 2019; personal visit to the Golden Valley marker, March 2, 2019; www.roadsideamerica.com/story/13833; www.minnpost.com/stroll/2014/12/45th-parallel-markers-make-note-minneapolis-distinction; www.

nationalgeographic.org/encyclopedia/latitude;
www.mnmuseumofthems.org; www.abbyplus.blogspot.com/2012/11/medicine-lakeand-45th-parallel.html.

68. **Magic of Skyrock**
Personal tour of Skyrock with Bill Nunn, April 23, 2019; www.mn.meetingsmags.com/skyrock-farm-carousel-hidden-gem-waiting-be-discovered; www.minnesota.cbslocal.com/2018/12/09/finding-minnesota-skyrock-farm; www.skyrockcarousel.com; www.skyrockfarm.com.

69. **Citywide Book of Poetry**
Email correspondences with Colleen Sheehy, president and executive director, Public Art Saint Paul, November 12, 2018 and June 19, 2019; www.twincities.com/2019/03/11/st-pauls-sidewalk-poetry-contest-returns-this-year-in-5-languages; www.publicartstpaul.org/about; www.indivisible.us/public-arts-st-paul; www.parkbugle.org/want-to-write-a-poem; www.minnpost.com/two-cities/2013/03/ifyou-think-youve-got-rhyme-its-st-paul-sidewalk-poetry-time; www.waterstonereview.com/sidewalk-poetry-small-moments-that-matter-by-amanda-happy.

70. **Insane Asylum Makeover**
Personal visit to the grounds, March 17, 2019; Email correspondence with Audra Hilse at the Anoka Historical Society, June 19, 2019; www.youtube.com/watch?v=1_NEITsPC0w; www.citypages.com/news/why-visiting-the-abandonedanoka-state-hospital-minnesotas-most-haunted-spot-is-a-bad-idea/397473581; www.startribune.com/historic-state-hospital-building-in-anoka-reopens-as-veteranshousing/463512033; www.startribune.com/fight-to-save-historic-anoka-buildingsbrings-renewed-push-for-veterans-housing/449789883; www.kstp.com/news/volunteers-convert-former-anoka-state-hospital-into-housing-for-veterans-eagleshealing-nest-/4704774; www.atlasobscura.com/places/anoka-state-hospital.

71. **"Oh, Good Grief!"**
Email correspondence with William Johnson, July 21, 2019; www.photodaves.com/peanuts/charlie/charliebrownlist.txt; www.johnweeks.com/tour/peanuts/charliebrown.html; www.schulzmuseum.org/about-schulz/schulz-biography; www.walkerart.org/minnesotabydesign/objects/peanuts; www.visitsaintpaul.com/blog/charles-m-schulz-saint-paul; www.startribune.com/schulz-remembers-the-early-daysin-minnesota-before-he-lived-on-peanuts/11475081.

72. **Fossil Fix**
Personal visit to ZRS Fossils and Gifts, March 20, 2019; Email correspondence with Kelly Lund, May 21, 2019; www.familyfuntwincities.com/dinosaurs-around-town; www.mprnews.org/story/2015/10/09/dinosaur-claw-minnesota-iron-range; www.startribune.com/fossil-adds-to-evidence-of-dinosaurs-in-minnesota/331496711; www.thoughtco.com/dinosaurs-and-prehistoric-animals-of-minnesota-1092081; www.minnpost.com/environment/2017/06/fossil-record-database-gives-insightminnesota-s-prehistoric-past.

73. **Seminary Surprise**
Personal visit to the chapel, April 16, 2019; Email correspondence with Paul Daniels, archivist and curator for Luther Seminary, May 31, 2019; www.collections.mnhs.org/MNHistoryMagazine/articles/38/v38i05p231-233.pdf; www.norwegianamerican.com/travel/a-piece-of-norway-close-to-home-st-paul-minnesotas-norwegiansurprise; www.luthersem.edu/archives/muskego.aspx; www.homesmsp.com/2011/03/walkable-st-anthony-park.html; www.atlasobscura.com/places/oldmuskego-church-2.

74. **Mound Builders**
Personal visit to Indian Mounds Regional Park, May 14, 2019; Nelson, Paul. "Indian Mounds Park, St. Paul." *MNopedia*, Minnesota Historical Society. www.mnopedia.org/place/indian-mounds-park-st-paul; Trimble, Steve. "What Is Known about the Indian Mounds?" Saint Paul Historical, www.saintpaulhistorical.com/items/show/184; Email correspondence with research center associate for the Ramsey County Historical Society; Phone discussion with longtime resident and RCHS editorial board member Steven Trimble, August 31, 2019; www.startribune.com/4-dakota-landmarks-hide-in-plain-sight-along-the-mississippi-river/491059421; www.stpaul.gov/facilities/

indian-mounds-regional-park; www.minnesotahistory.net/wptest/?p=4010; www.dakotahistory.org/images/history/South-St.-Paul-Voice-History-Archive-by-Lois-Glewwe.pdf.

75. **Northwest Nostalgia**
Email correspondence with Bruce Kitt, April 10, 2019; Personal visit to the museum; www.minnesota.cbslocal.com/2017/12/17/finding-mn-northwest-airlines-history-center; www.northwestairlineshistory.org/wp-content/uploads/2018/05/1609-newsletter.pdf; www.youtube.com/watch?v=DE8sxi80MCQ; www.mprnews.org/story/2008/01/09/nwa_history.

76. **Eighty-One Minutes**
Personal visit to the museum, July 13, 2019; www.discussions.mnhs.org/mnlocalhistory/blog/2012/05/15/firefighters-hall-and-museum; www.atlasobscura.com/places/firefighters-hall-and-museum; www.salaarc.com/blog/81-minutes-after-the-bridge-collapse; www.bluestemheritage.com/portfolio/81-minutes-after-the-bridge-collapse; www.mnhs.org/media/news/8746; www.hometownsource.com/elk_river_star_news/news/local/i--w-bridge-collapse-s-five-year-anniversary-nears/article_2b153081-4d40-57af-88e0-eb9ec9c2aa8c.html; www.johnweeks.com/i35w/i35w_garden.html.

77. **Tied Up in Knots**
Email correspondence with Reyn Guyer, July 10, 2019; www.thefactsite.com/2009/05/history-of-twister.html; www.reynguyer.com/ajax/pages/twister.html; www.todayifoundout.com/index.php/2013/08/the-slightly-sordid-history-of-twister; www.minnpost.com/twin-cities-business/2015/06/50-minnesota-innovations-changed-world.

78. **Skyway Scoop**
Email correspondence with Richard Rossi Sr., property manager, Madison Equities, Inc., April 8, 2019; Nathanson, Iric. "Minneapolis Skyways." *MNopedia*, Minnesota Historical Society, www.mnopedia.org/structure/minneapolis-skyways; www.minnpost.com/minnesota-history/2013/07/minneapolis-oldest-skyway-still-use-turns-50; www.atlasobscura.com/places/first-national-bank-building-skyway; www.minneapolis.org/map-transportation/minneapolis-skyway-guide; www.startribune.com/biggest-skyway-system-in-the-world-minneapolis-is-about-to-get-bigger/366130581; www.tripsavvy.com/st-pauls-skyway-system-2370010; www.m.startribune.com/the-good-the-bad-and-the-weird-in-minneapolis-skyways/466887213.

79. **Dayton's Monkey and Mementos**
Email correspondence with Cailin Rogers of Telos, lead developer for the Dayton's Project, August 2019; "Old Minneapolis," Facebook group; Nelson, Paul. "Dayton's." *MNopedia*, Minnesota Historical Society, www.mnopedia.org/group/dayton-s; www.mnhs.org/blog/collectionsupclose/8736; www.video.startribune.com/man-who-allegedly-stole-monkey-from-dayton-s-tells-his-tale/479522213; www.mnhs.org/blog/collectionsupclose/8736; www.foxnews.com/us/mummified-monkey-found-in-century-old-department-store-in-minnesota.

80. **Willy Wonkaish**
Email correspondence with Alex Allen from Pearson's Operations Department, August 6, 2019; www.pearsonscandy.com/history; www.minnesotamonthly.com/Blogs/Taste-Blog/April-2013/Pearson-Candy-Company-Tour; www.twincities.com/2009/05/27/minnesotas-own-pearsons-candy-co-turns-100-this-month; www.startribune.com/pearson-s-is-developing-a-new-candy-brand-named-for-its-st-paul-location/399336221; www.web.archive.org/web/20010302180916; citypages.com/databank/19/942/article6825.asp; www.tcbmag.com/news/articles/2013/minnesota-is-a-sweet-spot-for-candy-makers; www.twincities.com/2018/11/17/asweet-deal-sale-brings-pearsons-candy-ownership-back-to-minnesota.

81. **Mushrooms and Mobsters**
Email correspondence with Donna at Wabasha Street Caves, June 19, 2019; Park, Sharon. "Gangster Era in St. Paul, 1900–1936." *MNopedia*, Minnesota Historical Society. www.mnopedia.org/gangster-era-st-paul-1900-1936; Millett, Larry. 2007. *AIA Guide to the Twin Cities: The Essential Source on the Architecture of Minneapolis and Saint Paul*. Minnesota Historical Society; www.wabashastreetcaves.com; www.visitsaintpaul.com/discover-saint-paul/gangster-past/history; www.onlyinyourstate.com/minnesota/wabasha-street-caves-mn; www.ozy.com/goodsht/the-history-of-america-told-through-one-citys-street-caves/79608;

www.wanderthemap.com/2014/11/gangster-history-wabasha-street-caves;
www.lehmannfarms.com.

82. **Airport Potty Pride**
Email correspondences with Ben Owen, director, Airport Foundation MSP, April 30, May 16, and
August 2, 2019; Phone interview with artist Mercedes Austin, October 9, 2018;
www.airportfoundation.org/programs-services/arts-culture/commissionedartwork/restrooms;
www.mercurymosaics.com/blogs/news/msp-airport-votedamerica-8217-s-best-restroom;
www.mymspconnect.com/news/201507/seeking-mosaic-artists; www.mspflymag.
com/2016/06/30/video-creating-mosaicwall-art-at-msp; www.bizjournals.com/twincities/
news/2016/11/21/msp-airportbathrooms-voted-best-in-america.html; www.startribune.com/
potty-polls-are-inmsp-wins-america-s-best-bathroom/402284265.

83. **Largest Raspberry**
www.hopkinsmn.com/514/History-of-the-Hopkins-Raspberry; www.m.startribune.com/hopkins-
returns-to-its-roots-and-plants-raspberries/382555151; www.highwayhighlights.com/2018/09/
worlds-largest-raspberry-hopkins-mn/

84. **Fitz Land**
Self-guided tour of a few of Fitzgerald's stomping grounds and the F. Scott Fitzgerald Reading
Alcove, May 28, 2010; Koblas, John J. 2004. *A Guide to F. Scott Fitzgerald's Saint Paul*. Minnesota
Historical Society; www.fitzgeraldinsaintpaul.org/a-selectionof-saint-paul-sites-of-f-scott-
fitzgerald; www.nytimes.com/2016/05/01/travel/f-scottfitzgerald-st-paul.html; www.history.
com/news/10-things-you-may-not-know-about-fscott-fitzgerald; www.saintpaulhistorical.com/
items/show/119.

85. **Corner Lot Diver**
Countless drive-bys; Phone interview with Jack Gause, early May 2019; Email correspondence
with Jack Gause's wife, Delores, July 10, 2019, three days after Jack passed away;
www.communitycelebration.org/elder/gause.

86. **Mega Move**
www.bizjournals.com/twincities/stories/1998/10/26/story2.html; www.thecowlescenter.org/
about-cowles/history-mission/history-shubert-theatre-goodaletheater; www.minneapolismn.
gov/hpc/landmarks/hpc_landmarks_hennepin_ave_516_shubert_theater; www.science.
howstuffworks.com/engineering/structural/heaviest-building-moved1.htm.

87. **A Snazzier Snelling**
Email correspondence with Jonathan Oppenheimer, April 11, 2019; www.tcdailyplanet.net/
murals-bridge-divides-snelling-avenue-saint-pauls-busieststreet; www.monitorsaintpaul.com/
midway-arts-festival; www.minnpost.com/arts-culture/2015/08/midway-murals-project-
beautifying-busy-snelling-avenuepublic-art; www.minneapolis.org/things-to-do/arts-culture/
murals-public-art; www.visitsaintpaul.com/blog/6-mysaintpaul-public-art-spots-to-check-out;
www.midwaymurals.com; www.womenspress.com/Content/Features/Featured/Article/Midway-
Murals-Project-/1/233/5094.

88. **Retro Repository**
Self-guided tour of the museum, August 21, 2019; Email correspondence with Sylvie Skoog,
August 29, 2019; www.facebook.com/pavekmuseum; www.youtube.com/watch?v=JzREheuvi44.

89. **Winged Ambassadors**
Email correspondence with Julia Ponder, executive director, University of Minnesota College of
Veterinary Medicine, August 16, 2019; Personal visit to The Raptor Center, July 28, 2019;
www.raptor.umn.edu.

90. **Bus Stop Bouquet**
Visited the bus stop May 13, 2019; www.blogs.mprnews.org/state-of-the-arts/2011/11/
sound-point-blossoms-of-hope; blogs.www.mprnews.org/state-of-the-arts/2011/11/sound-
point-blossoms-of-hope; www.startribune.com/may-22-2011-deadly-tornado-crashes-through-
north-minneapolis/122417279; www.inhabitat.com/duo-gards-blossoms-of-hope-bus-shelter-
sprouts-in-minneapolis.

INDEX